Message Ahead

Message Ahead

Poets Respond to the Poems of Jonas Mekas

John Godfrey
Yoshimasu Gōzō
Barry Schwabsky
Charity Coleman
James Sherry
William Benton
Kimberly Lyons
Krzysztof Czyżewski
Lina Vitkauskas
Brenda Iijima
Yuko Otomo
Basil King
Steve Dalachinsky
Carter Ratcliff
Kristin Prevallet
George Quasha
Bob Holman
Benjamin Sloan
Lee Ann Brown
& Louise Landes Levi
Penny Arcade
Sparrow

Edited by Vyt Bakaitis

RAIL EDITIONS BROOKLYN, NEW YORK

Contents

A Timeline

A timeline for the books of poems by Jonas Mekas under consideration, listing first the year of composition and original Lithuanian publication and then the later appearance in English:

1948	*Idylls of Semeniškiai*, translated by Vyt Bakaitis, in *There Is No Ithaca*, Black Thistle Press: 1996
	Idylls of Semeniškiai, translated by Adolfas Mekas, Hallelujah Editions: 2007
1951/ 1972	*Reminiscences*, in *There Is No Ithaca*, translated by Vyt Bakaitis, Black Thistle Press: 1996
1967	*Words Apart and Others*, translated by Vyt Bakaitis, Rail Editions: 2018
1985	*Daybooks 1970-72*, translated by Vyt Bakaitis, Portable Press at Yo-Yo Labs: 2003

Vyt Bakaitis
For Openers

Poetry speaks for itself, but we don't know this until the poet finds a voice to say it.

Time in its ongoing verdict predisposes a factual trail one should be able to follow, if only in order to expand from the start on a minimal context, exclusively individual and routinely existential. Yet over time everything changes, and as language evolves, and individual experience fluctuates, much of the truth of experience will escape meaning, while the truth of a poem will show more than words can say. Such is the double bind of mystery and ambiguity in the progression the poet then works to resolve into a common bond, a fusion that might link the word to the world. By a canny aside in *Victory*, one of his later novels, Joseph Conrad came to sum up the whole winding, shifting process as "the charm of art tense with life."

Over his long lifetime, Jonas Mekas has adhered to a radical aesthetic of openness, and the poetry he has made into books and films posts clear-cut markers along the trail as his journey continues. Since 1922, the year of his birth in an economically depressed Lithuanian countryside, he has kept his eyes and ears open. He could read and write by the age of five and had his first poems published in local newspapers by mid-adolescence. He carried and kept his writings with him through an inordinate wartime dislocation into Germany—under conditions no better than the swarms of refugees today find themselves in—and having settled in a postwar UN camp for stateless refugees Mekas wrote and had published his first book of poems, which was soon acknowledged as a classic of Lithuanian letters. On reaching New York in 1949, he started gradually developing a celebrated career as filmmaker and promoter of independent film, yet he also continued in each of the next four decades to create a book of new poems in Lithuanian. Right now he is getting ready to release the first book of poems he has written in English, tentatively titled *The Book of Her*.

The poet Jonas Mekas creates durable works, and fellow poets gather here to appraise, for clarity and currency, certain of the poems he has published.

That these poets took on the challenge to fathom intently the riddle in the older texts makes me glad and grateful to each of them; and gratified twice over that they could see through the translations—whether done by me or by Adolfas Mekas—to find real evidence of the poem.

During a blackout, when one steps into a room long familiar, inching gropingly along, a struck match at once redefines bearings, yet the new light now reveals the well-known objects as if not seen before, each with its own halo of shading.

Let our senses send up signals for spirit to engender, like smoke from open fires the wind whirls into shape before our smarting eyes.

VYT BAKAITIS has two books of poems, *City Country* (Black Thistle Press, 1992) and *Deliberate Proof* (Lunar Chandelier, 2010), with current work online in *Cafe Review* and *Local Knowledge*. Others of his translations from Lithuanian make up the bilingual poetry anthology he edited, *Breathing Free* (Lithuanian Writers' Union/ Spuyten Duyvil, 2002).

John Godfrey

Jonas Mekas

Memory is an organelle of imagination, a sizeable chip in the mind's hard drive, a place where fantasy and demoralization can both be found, where a fleckless vision of reality meets tangent dark personal history, where facts are altered and fiction is embraced. The dress she wore the first time we met was blue, I swear, but she still has that red dress she had bought just for the occasion. Memory can be a high or a low, and one believes it.

One writes poems, say. Jonas Mekas has for more than 70 years. One's first inspirations form the poetry skeleton that permits movement and dexterity throughout the writing life. How enduring are the first influences? How conscious or subliminal are they? What was the poet's first self-image as a poet? Then there's the poet's character. How willing or unwilling is the poet to change ideas? How willing or unwilling to continue the tried and true?

The poet's first impulse in writing—impulse both as a mental stimulus in reaction to an existence in certain environs, and impulse as the desire to emulate inherited writing and even the spiritual outlooks of earlier and contemporary writers—leaves genetic traces in the poet's literary skeleton. That skeleton is Ithaca, and when one returns there the dog recognizes you, and the story ends. When one is reduced by time to the bones, stilled and shortened by age, that compact genetic evidence comes to the poet as a shorthand transcription.

One is fortunate to have a longtime home to remember, one that provides the bone works, the naked skeleton of one's being. The structure on which one hangs the experiences of a lifetime.

Twenty-five is a tender age, Mekas's when he had finished *Idylls of Semeniškiai*, which I know from Vyt Bakaitis's translation in *There Is No Ithaca* (Black Thistle Press, 1996). From the "First Idyll" and never relenting, Mekas writes with the excitement of making word choices. The writing carries an epic sort of heatedness, the vitality of folklore. The poet induces in himself the vision of what he describes; he describes it in the present indicative. By keeping the vision alive he prevents that world from being something that was. There is something Homerically elegiac in his wish.

Each idyll could be a film scenario. There are few generalities and many modifiers, and these modifiers have a vignette-like quality. The natural world is described in vivid verbs and rustic adjectives. The humans lead lives regulated by nature, whose harshness is rendered in very precise verbs and sensorial detail. A touch of social realism, a touch of Latin pastoral. The young poet lets out his breath, all inclusive. The camera roves, putting this world in front of you. The poem as screen, as panorama, the Lithuanian is full of alliterative vowel endings and a rhythmic scan free from fixed meter or rhyme. (Bakaitis confirmed this in conversation.)

"First Idyll" all but refers to Kristijonas Donelaitis by name. I know parts of Donelaitis's seasonal poems from Bakaitis's *Breathing Free: Poems from the Lithuanian* (Lithuanian Writers' Union Publishers, Vilnius, 2002). Donelaitis writes in metaphors and Bakaitis has told me that Donelaitis, a cosmopolitan man, had the intent of using Lithuanian in a Virgilian, latinated way. It seems as if Mekas intends to answer this in the rustic, observant and vigilant way of a countryman. And Mekas is genuinely a country person. He tells you what the color of bark means during the course of the seasons, and he names the tree. He chooses the biblical tone as if describing the creation of the world. He begins, "Old is rain gushing down shrubstems, / cockgrouse drumming in the red summer dawn. / Old is our talk of this." ("First Idyll")

Plant life, atmospheric changeability, and livestock are made plainly visible. Human activity is described through tasks. The folks' sentiments and psychology are only slightly implied. Humans are depicted as a small part of the natural world. "Idyll Four" is a subtle cradle-to-grave ballad. It begins with "A fresh smell of woods, pine-sap and timber / breezes in each spring, past chill rain screens" as if these are the very first memories of an infant. The poem is directed to a "you" who could be the infant who becomes a child through sensorial experience, but who could also be the slim women of the fields. The poem concludes with a summation of the life cycle. The child's tactile awakening, followed by intimations of desire in girls, followed by a coffin in the parlor and then in the ground. The ending suggests particulars that death leaves behind: "Lush meadows in blossom. Clean-smelling loam. / Neighing stallions. Resounding, partying Saturday nights. / The yellow maplewood spoon." What a genius last three lines!

Mekas takes especial pains in putting the power of water into words. "Seventh Idyll" describes the violence of a thunderstorm with awe. The downpour becomes tumbling diction—"rousing harsh," "gushing," "drubbing," "slashing," "felling," "chopping" and "lashing." "Twentieth Idyll" treats of the aftermath of long rains—"as though each pace is bound to take forever, / a farmer walks in step with his fate . . ."

The writing seems to yearn for control—reality described in the perfect words in order to control it, as an edited film can. And what we see on the screen of words is, in fact, the depiction of reality as in control and importuning. The human reality in each idyll has its own kind of controls, communal labor, and the expression of family through household duties. A constant is the smell, sound, and appearance of a thriving, hard life in life-giving detail. No sentimentality, no judgments. No human secrets revealed. There is nothing here for which to forgive humans.

Reminiscences, which follows the *Idylls* in *There Is No Ithaca*, was completed in 1951, after Mekas had reached Brooklyn. I know it from Bakaitis's translation. In it, Mekas seems to ask a different question of poetry. If the *Idylls* had asked if a poem could recreate the active life in nature, *Reminiscences* asks how a long poem sequence can relate the drawn-out displaced experience that left Mekas for years moving through Europe with other displaced persons from Lithuania. The change in the writing is from inspired lyricism to narration. The frequently breathless quality of the *Idylls* becomes a well-paced remembrance of persons and their circumstances. The fellowship of farm tasks is here the community of the homeless. The writing is less concerned with being distinctive in itself, with virtuosity. I do not read Lithuanian but in looking at the poem's structure in the Lithuanian I'm guessing there is serious concern for musicality and recurring end-sounds. It is, in fact, a song, and these changes in Mekas's writing are more suited to the song from the memory, from the heart. This could be the effect of remembering so much helplessness and unpredictability. The writing throughout *Reminiscences* is almost completely in the past tense, which lends a more languid tone. Time is compressed in the narrative, and there is a disregard for meticulously detailed visuals except as attached in rhythmic clusters of precision related to destruction, colors, wind, and rain. The first poem comes close to the visual fervor of the *Idylls*, but succeeding sections are meditative and narrative. Here, humans and the poet's love of their companionship are treated meditatively. The simplicity and artless feeling are universal, but it is the simplicity that is necessary for it to be credible. This is sincerity. Sincerity is voluntary and without resistance and in a sense not part of reality. But it is true to feeling. The fellowship of the displaced is related as a melancholy buoyancy. The grueling parts of their existence are referred to briefly in passing. What is chosen to be remembered recounts what Mekas misses then, in Brooklyn, and what rural New York brings to mind in the later sections. Nostalgia for nature, in the *Idylls*, becomes nostalgia for shared human experience. Without sentimentality Mekas sings of sorrow. Brooklyn has made an end of the lyric loftiness of youth but not at the expense of an expansive—American—soul. The American soul has shallow roots. Mekas suggests this in his dwelling on memories, for he will not have deep memories of America, in America. The experience of New York is fresh but he seems to be letting go of the displaced post-war experience. The last poems of the sequence make it clear that America is a new displaced experience. It is only in the closing section that the poet situates himself in America, looking at the upstate New York countryside as echoes of "home," and looking to fellow countrymen in America for the bond of home:

> Home. Home. Each place,
> each horizon, meeting and face:
> each stop to look
> a tie to home.

"Namai" in Lithuanian seems a more feeling word than "home." Like an actual name. The cycle ends in "Sorrow, sorrow, sorrow." Sorrow in Lithuanian, "vargas," is a fittingly plaintive sound.

In 1972 Mekas returned from a visit to his mother and his childhood home, Semeniškiai. He made a stunning film from the visit, *Reminiscences of a Journey to Lithuania*, including frames in which the camera lolls about like a head on shoulders. There are lightning-fast edits, shots of fields and trees that are full of the details drawn out in the *Idylls*, but here to be apprehended in an instant. Characteristically, the edits allow longer takes of faces. Over all, the film is in shorthand.

Begun around the time of that trip and continuing to 1980, Mekas wrote the poems—seventy-six of them—translated by Vyt Bakaitis as *Daybooks 1970 – 72* (Portable Press at Yo-Yo Labs, 2003). This is a fundamentally different poet. In the prior two collections, Mekas had written memories as if being himself in memory. As if displacing himself from the person sitting in reality writing the poem. In *Daybooks*, which indeed speaks of memories, there is now no illusion that the person writing can any longer enter memory. As if, for him, memory and vegetation were bonded. Poem "12" begins:

> So:
> civilization has no poetry,
> I've slipped
>   away from nature.

Poem "12" states that for him the poetry is the past, and that for him the past is nature. Without nature, poetry withers and is swept away by time.

When writing these poems, Mekas had for two decades surely registered the impact of Asian poetry and philosophy on the most advanced artists of the time. In Confucian and Buddhist thought the emphasis is on the present and in honesty with the self. There are poems that recall Tu Fu's great poems of exile and remembrance (39, 49, 52). In *Daybooks* there is always the feeling that the person writing is in the present, yet Mekas refers to memories often, now with a tone of alienation. He is, after all, literally alien in New York. Writing as if in the actual present he matches the tone of alienation with lines that are short, poems of few words, a good bit of acerbity, and an honesty completely distinguishable from the sincerity of twenty years earlier. Writing in the moment, his depressions and isolation color almost every poem. Now there is drama, the idealistic wanderer knows he meets resistance. (The idealistic loser, I might add, was a cultural figure in the American '50s, '60s, and '70s.) The poet is begrudgingly assimilated.

And these poems are up to date for the times. Grammar is eliminated in many poems. Several are entirely in lower case. If grammar and observance of standard typography are like editing film, these poems bear a great resemblance to his techniques of juxtaposition and brevity in choosing from footage.

61.

roadside icon
hilltop cross
heart of a bell

the field rye
the linden limb
the forest moss

city gates
dusty footpath
blood duct

viper's foam.

I get the feeling from these poems that Mekas is influenced by his filmmaking esthetics. Brevity, vividness, and a view that wobbles just as his camera does. Film is also a way of sustaining the moment, to put memory in front of one repeatedly. In the poems he is more honest, his mind seems more real, and his despairing idealism is more moving. Memory is the skeleton of this poet and in *Daybooks* his estrangement from memories, which is my reading of the laconic and regretful tone, gives Mekas for the first time the conflict and doubt—resistances—that add to his art that extra on-the-edgeness to make this collection his best and most contemporary work. The poet asks the poem to capture the world in a different, smaller way. He now writes from an historical present at a time when memories are cruelly difficult to enter. His bare bones.

JOHN GODFREY became acquainted with the New York idea of writing poems in 1965. He has lived in the East Village since the end of the '60s. On three occasions over the years he has led workshops at the Poetry Project at St. Mark's. The 14th of his collections to be published is *The City Keeps: New and Selected Poems 1966–2014* (Wave Books, 2016).

"As humans exhaust all the possible depredations that can be committed by beliefs, the earth is proving that she belongs to the earth. We have colonized her and she will overthrow us violently in a war of liberation unless radical acts of divestment and concession are realized, not just considered."

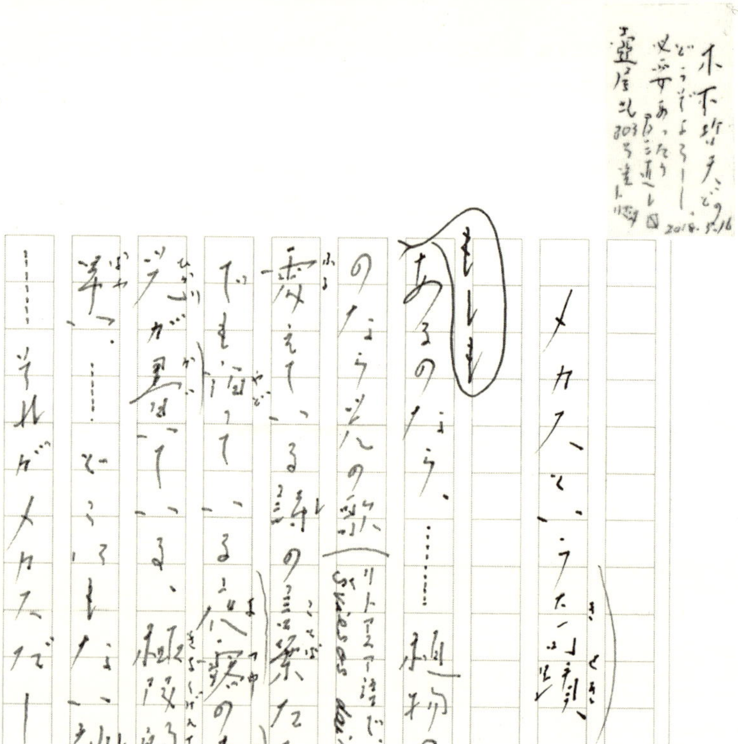

Yoshimasu Gōzō: Manuscript, in Japanese, of “The Miracle That Is Mekas.”

Yoshimasu Gōzō

The Miracle That Is Mekas

If only, then . . . Barefoot roots of plants, if only, then bare feet in the depths of a song of lights (Lithuanian: *šviesų daina*) . . . Bare feet of nighttime dew residing persistently on the stalks and on the branches and the leaves of quivering words of poetry . . . The infinitely anxious and infinitely rapid, surely scribed by the glow of wounds . . . Bare feet of a quicksilver gaze neither here nor there . . . This, Mekas!

—*Translated into English by Waku Miller*

YOSHIMASU GŌZŌ is a Japanese poet who has several books in English translation: *Devil's Wind: A Thousand Steps or More* (1980), *Osiris: the God of Stone* (1989), and most recently *Alice, Iris, Red Horse: Selected Poems* (2016). He is widely known for the public readings he has done as performances of creative improvisation, often in collaboration with jazz musicians.

Barry Schwabsky
A Note on Cinematic Time and Poetry

When I first visited Lithuania in 2008 and the name of Jonas Mekas came up, I was surprised to be told that his work as a filmmaker was hardly known in his homeland, but that as a poet he was famous. I had known of him first as a film critic, then as a filmmaker, and I still hadn't read his poetry, though I had an inkling it existed. Since then I've learned more. I know enough to see Czesław Miłosz's point when he wrote of Mekas as "both a poet and a poet of things observed and preserved on the film reel"—his cinema is poetic and his poetry is cinematic. Even his earliest poems, before he ever thought of picking up a movie camera, can be read as sequences of images, scripts for non-narrative films. Consider the first of his *Idylls of Semeniškiai*:

> Old is rain gushing down shrubstems,
> cockgrouse drumming in the red summer dawn.

There you have not only a sequence of images, each formed of separate shots (I imagine the rain as a long shot, then a close-up of the stems, followed by another close-up, this time of the fowl, leading to another long shot of the sun rising over the wet landscape—a sort of cinematic chiasmus) but the sound track to go with them—the gushing and the drumming. In the poem's third line—"Old is our talk of this"—I hear something new coming into the sound track: a murmuring of voices. Perhaps the words can't quite be made out. What matter? It's old talk, talk of things long since spoken of and spoken again, and what matters is that the tone of it is the tone of familiarity, of home.

The flux of images continues, works itself by association through the multitude of sights that make of the life of farmers, the whole round of seasons, from the summer that's been mentioned in the poem's second line through "lonesome autumn" through "white winter glare"—but the seasons don't return in order: Between autumn and winter comes "the heavy summer heat," and after the winter we hear again of "autumn, while fields turn gray," of "roads, in October, washed out and swamped." But spring is not mentioned; it is being held in reserve for the second idyll, "How Spring Smells," which begins the more linear traversal of the yearly cycle that follows in the rest of the sequence.

The talk of this round of seasons and the tasks it brings with it, the old, murmuring talk, is implicitly of the present, though in fact the images are without tense, that is, without verbs (except as part of noun phrases):

> And of the fields, yellowing barley and oats,
> the cowherd fires wetblown in lonesome autumn.
> Of the potato digs,
> the heavy summer heat,
> white winter glare and sleigh-din down unending roads.

—and so on. Perhaps this is also part of the cinematic nature of these sights and sounds, that they are timelessly present. The cinema knows no tenses except by way of certain artifices that always feel a bit false and a bit naïve, and which here the poet eschews: the flashback is always seen by the audience as a present occurrence.

But the poem finds it as hard to live without tenses as the film finds it hard to live with them. The "long generations / pacing the fields off, wearing down plowland," are innumerable, and encompass not only those alive today, but the people of the past, the "fathers." They, the fathers, are the subject of the next part of the poem, and their time, their tense, is the past:

> Out of these cool stone wells
> they drew water for their returning herds,
> and when the flooring in the place wore down,
> or the housewall quietly started to crumble,
> they dug their yellow clay from the same pits,
> their sand gold-fresh from the same fields.

But this is a special kind of past tense, it seems. One hardly feels it as past. Everything seems so immediate—"gold-fresh." We see the herds, the crumbling wall, the clay pit. Even as past, they are present. And then later, too, the poet says,

> there will be others, sitting on blue fieldstones,
> mowing the overgrown meadows, plowing these plains,
> and when they come in at the end of their day and sit
> down to the tables,
> each table, each clay jug,
> each beam in the wall will speak,
> they'll have the sprawling yellow sandbanks to remember,
> and ryefields swaying in the wind,
> the sad songs of our women from the far side of a flax field,
> and one smell, on first entering a new parlor,
> the scent of fresh moss!

There is a future tense that, like the past tense of this poem, is such in a special sense. This future is already here, it is the wholly known, the wholly already-present; we can see before us "the sprawling yellow sandbanks" of this future.

The cyclical time of this peasant existence is a temporality unrecognizable to modern urban life. Because it is cyclical time, it returns to itself, and the poem ends as it began, with the old rain gushing down the shrubstems and the cockgrouse drumming and the self-confirming assertion that "Old is our talk of all this"—self-affirming because we recognize it as something we have already heard before, already known.

Here I have to register my surprise at Miłosz's praise of Mekas's "sensitivity to unrepeatable light, color, scents of his native region," for if Mekas himself is to be believed, all these things—the light, the color, the scents (and as I said, the sounds)—are endlessly repeatable. Just as the reel can be replaced on the projector and the film screened again (and this repeatability is precisely of the essence of the film, which Walter Benjamin famously hailed as "the work of art in the age of its technical reproducibility"), so the life of peasants is an endless round of repeated activities. And yet each time something is repeated, it is renewed. It wears down, it crumbles, and it is refreshed. This present is eternal effort, a laborious renewal of what was so that it will be. The reel must be rerun.

But like most movies, the reel is a fiction. As Mekas wrote in *I Had Nowhere to Go*, his memoir of his time in Germany, first as prisoner in a forced labor camp and then as a displaced person, followed by his arrival and early years in New York: "I know nothing about my father's early life. Or that of my mother's. I never asked them about it. I know only a few very general facts. I have never seen my grandfather. I presume he was a farmer." In fact, he says: "I didn't know who my nieces or cousins or aunts were or any other relative of any kind. My ancestors were all the living and dead poets, philosophers, encyclopedists."

The *Idylls of Semeniškiai* in their U.S. publication commence with the notation of their place and date of publication: "1948 Kassel." For reasons that can only be described as bitterly ironic, Mekas had inadvertently found his way to the land of the poets and philosophers (if not of the encyclopedists) and the poem implicitly shows it, with its evocation of the table, the jug, the beam that might well have meet the approval of that Rilke who asked: "Are we here perhaps just to say: house, bridge, well, gate, jug, fruit tree, window?" or of that Heidegger (referred to scathingly in passing by Mekas in *I Had Nowhere to Go*) who in 1950 would observe: "The jug is not a vessel because it was made; rather, the jug had to be made because it is this holding vessel." That is to say, the *Idylls* are the writings of a displaced person, someone who has been displaced above all from the life described in the poems—displaced first by himself as one whose horizon of thought extended far beyond the immediate life embodied in the jug, the wall, the tended field, and then more violently by politics and its continuation by other means as war. Both thought and war reveal the solidity of the peasant's existence as illusory, and the vision of poets and philosophers as equally fragile though no less precious for that.

Perhaps, then, those "long generations" of which he writes, the peasants "pacing the fields off, wearing down plowland," represent those who plow metaphorical fields, the fields of thought. And yet, Mekas says, "all my ancestors have been farmers." The content of the poem is a nostalgia for a way of life from which Mekas had to depart in order to become the poet and filmmaker he is—a way of life that is in part imaginary but that offers material for arts in which it must be that "each table, each clay jug, / each beam in the wall will speak," which are the ones that Mekas practiced. "All the romantics praised it," he notes of the life of the farmer, and he is among their number.

BARRY SCHWABSKY is art critic for *The Nation* and coeditor of international reviews for Artforum. His recent books are *Heretics of Language* (Black Square Editions, 2018), *The Perpetual Guest: Art in the Unfinished Present* (Verso, 2016), and a collection of poetry, *Trembling Hand Equilibrium* (Black Square Editions, 2015).

"**Uninformed is he who would proclaim himself his own contemporary, deserting or usurping with equal imprudence, when the past seems to cease and the future to stall, in view of masking the gap.**" (Stéphane Mallarmé)

Charity Coleman
A Place for a Bird

I went to Jonas's house to be interviewed for the job of editing and proofreading some of his writings. As we discussed business, I realized that he was not very interested in my employment history (and neither was I).

Finally, I said: "... and I write poetry."

He perked up: "Ah! you write poetry! *That* is why you are good for the job."

"The job" was supposed to take a few weeks. I worked with Jonas for three and a half years, on five books.

One of my favorite lines of his (there are many) comes from his early diary entries (1958)—

> *"Who knows what the songs of the birds do to the earth during the spring."*

Tidy words, a simple sentence that pulls you in for a closer look. I wrote it on a post-it note and stuck it to the window by his desk, where it stayed for several seasons.

He appears in my dreams: often eating, carousing, being a poet, always a friend.

> Me: "I had a long dream about you this weekend. You were

reciting poetry in your big fancy house and you had a sign on the front door that said SAINT THOMAS."
Jonas: "I dreamt I was eating raspberries."

Jonas lives a great poem. He doesn't say anything that doesn't need to be said, and what needs to be said gets said only as it ought! He once responded to a poem of mine by saying what should also be said about all of HIS poetry, so I will speak about HIS poetry using HIS words which are the best words for the job:

Jonas Mekas's poetry is . . .

> *". . . daydreaming in reality, out of reality and at the same time very very real where there is a place even for a bird—and when I read it, it made me feel good and at the same time I knew I was reading a poem that had roots in all good, great poetry—personal and impersonal"*

CHARITY COLEMAN is the author of a forthcoming collection of essays and elegies, and *Julyiary* (O'clock Press). Her writing has appeared in *BOMB*, *Brooklyn Rail*, *Prelude*, *Dolce Stil Criollo*, *Fanzine*, *Entropy*, and elsewhere. She lives in NYC.

"The freezer is full of compost and soft gold glitter called a life that fills a body, speaking back to the interim."

James Sherry
Mekas's Idylls

It's 1964 and I'm into experimental film. So where do I go but the Cinematheque? I don't remember exactly, I think 41st Street was the location. At this early point in my life, I don't know about avant-garde traditions or who is sitting around me, so I may be in august company. It's a dark place, and it smells dank.

But I'm fascinated by these short films where young men sit in trees, glowering at me. Why are they sitting there? And some slow pans of industrial wasteland have encouraged my lifelong fascination with cars coming around corners, their doors opening—then a person gets out to go into a building. I remember Kenneth Anger's examination of corruption. I wish I had more context on this memory, but then it was all about looking at the film really hard and trying to figure out why people bothered to do these long slow takes of fingers; it seemed perverse not to get on with it. And there's some relationship between this place and a fabled individual named Jonas Mekas.

Now, thanks to the amazing Vyt Bakaitis's translations of the Lithuanian poems, we know a lot more about Jonas Mekas, not just the filmography, but much of the poetry and journals. A more complete picture of Mekas, the person, distinguished from the art-world figure, is vital to understanding the postwar art scene in New York. So many people came back from war, sought a society that avoided war, appeared in the US for the first time having escaped the war, or came back to an America that now looked alien. I want to float the thought that there was a strong tendency in postwar abstraction and avant-gardism toward displacement. Certainly, in Jonas's case, his fleeing through Europe and eventually landing in the US must have influenced his work and his choice of the works to promote through the Cinematheque.

Take, for example, these entries from his ongoing journal. Mekas, the poet, at first finds himself in a strange world:

> We felt the pull of distance.
> War was just over, with its last
> shells, its last bomb blasts
> still echoing off the slopes. Past stations in rubble,
> and gutted, charred little towns,
> we kept moving on, pushing our way in
> among women and children,
> war prisoners and miserable soldiers
> squatted down in muggy heat, slumped together
> with the swarms of refugees
> on grimy floors . . .[1]

And later on, in December 1951, the diarist registers the alienation he feels on arriving in America:

> But I remain a stranger here. There is a distance between me and every building, every street, every face.[2]

This is not the voice of resistance, or how Americans typically interpreted its postwar art. Mekas's vision is far from Clement Greenberg's statement about Hans Hoffman's "dissolution of the subject"[3] or Harold Rosenberg's article "The American Action Painters" that told about "revelation."[4] Yet Mekas's vision includes resistance in his activities in Europe, a part of his rerouting:

> During the years 1943 – 1944, during which time Lithuania was under German occupation, I got involved, like many other people my

age, in various anti-German activities. I joined a small underground group which, amongst other things, was publishing a weekly underground bulletin.[5]

The thought process of the filmmaker / poet appears here as more circumspect and judicious than the *enfant terrible* of Anger and others critiquing Hollywood. Mekas, revealing his later penchant for producing institutions and events, writes objectively about the trauma of passing through the ravages of war and at the same time is actively involved in resistance. This combination of misery, displacement, and resistance is visible in many of the films that Mekas made and presented in his serial institutions.

Yet as Jan-Christopher Horak says in his essay:

> It seems to me that while the artist and the object have been privileged in critical discourses surrounding avant-garde film and its historiography, it is often wrongly assumed that modernism eludes subject positioning altogether because the mechanisms of identification so well defined in relation to classical Hollywood narrative are completely subverted in avant-garde film practice.[6]

To me this combination of grounded subjectivity—by which I mean you lose any airy idea of yourself when ground down to a nub of existence by war and suffering—and active resistance is embodied by filmmakers such as Kenneth Anger, Stan Brakhage, Maya Deren, Hollis Frampton, and continues through the next generation of filmmakers who follow them. Even the surfaces of minimalists like Michael Snow and Ernie Gehr reflect this combination of grounded subjectivity and resistance.

Mekas, always at the center of this hybrid organism, drives his model of displacement through his poetry. In this instance, he reverts to a prewar idyllic mode for a moment indicative of his later work; in the *Reminiscences*, for example, which he set down first in 1951 and published only twenty years later in 1972:

> Dizzy with summer blossoming,
> all that vitality, that vineland fragrance,
> we sat there on a hillside looking down
> the deep track the stream of the Neckar had carved . . .[7]

And the idyllic pervades each of the earlier *Idylls* from 1948, as in "Eleventh Idyll":

> Oh and the wind's touch, lukewarm mist,
> rain drubbing the roof,
> leaves rustling, tremulous aspen jitters,
> autumn rain in the pines,
> a swallow flying by,
> taproots gnawing the ground deeper down:
> each of these makes a shimmer all its own.[8]

These nature poems revert to the lost landscape of his Lithuanian youth. They might be eco-poetical investigations, new nature poems from Jonathan Skinner, had they not leapt across what has been nearly seventy years since Mekas left his rural Baltic landscape. And rather than reify eco-poetry's false binary of humanity and nature, Mekas's environmental model includes what Michael Pollan calls "second nature,"[9] the human ordering of non-human life.

> The fields look stripped, except where the rows
> stretch lone and pale, out in the stubble
> and the newly tilled fallow;

now somewhere nearby, not far from the slumped cottage . . .[10]

Acknowledging the connection between people and other parts of the biosphere as another order, *Idylls* continually reconnects with the lost youthful energy of the poet's homeland. The reader alternates between empathy with these sentiments, frozen in their high-definition detail, and a Romanticism reminiscent of the Lake Poets; who already had, if not exclusively by way of Villon's resonant "*ou sont les neiges d'antan*" (where are the snows of yesteryear) refrain, recharged a common link back to the late-Latin "*ubi sunt*" (where are they) motif, that was prevalent among medieval poets across several cultures and has its clear echo in this latter-day variant by Mekas:

> Where are you now, my old friends,
> you I grew up with
> close as the bushes, fields, and sandbanks:
> where are you, and those fields,
> the flax-retting pools and the high summer sky?
> And that December snow?[11]

Modernism and retrouvé landscape. As John Ashbery said, in commending the translation of the *Idylls* by Adolfas Mekas:

> Nature, all but unmediated, pulses through the poems of recollected childhood . . . in free-verse "idylls" that recall Virgil's *Georgics*, Hölderlin, Stifter, Clare, Leopardi, Rilke, Pasternak, and William Carlos Williams, and are as direct as cinematography. His brother, and fellow cineaste Adolfas, who was with him in exile and had shared those Kinderszenen, has performed a valuable service by rendering these marvelous poems in a crystalline translation whose clarity and emotional nuance are that of memory itself. *Idylls of Semeniškiai* is a spellbinding work of collaboration.[12]

When we think about those years, we remember the anger and resistance against the establishment, rising into the counterculture. We might remember as well Mekas's delicate retrieval of a lost, idyllic world that with global corporatism expanding, like Anger's *Scorpio Rising*, has all but disappeared.

Endnotes

1 *There Is No Ithaca*, tr. Vyt Bakaitis, Black Thistle Press, New York, 1996, p. 119.

2 Jonas Mekas as quoted in Jan-Christopher Horak, "Rereading Mekas: Avant-garde Film andAudience Subjectivity," http://mfj-online.org/journalPages/MFJ53/Horak.html, 11/26/17.

3 Clement Greenberg, "The Crisis of the Easel Picture," *Art and Culture*, Beacon Press, Boston, 1961; the article, which first appeared in *Partisan Review*, 1948, echoes Hofmann's "dissolution of the subject" saying, "the dissolution of the pictorial into sheer texture, into apparently sheer sensation, into an accumulation of repetitions, seems to speak for and answer something profound in contemporary sensibility."

4 Harold Rosenberg, "The American Action Painters," *The Tradition of the New*, 1959, first appeared in *Art News*, December, 1952.

5 Jonas Mekas, *I Had Nowhere to Go* (Black Thistle Press, 1991), as quoted in Gary Comenas, "Jonas Mekas and the Film-Makers' Cinematheque" (2014), http://www.warholstars.org/filmmakers-cinematheque-1-1961-62.html, 11/25/17.

6 Horak, op. cit.

7 Jonas Mekas, *Reminiscences*, op. cit., p. 129.

8 Jonas Mekas, *Idylls of Semeniskiai* (1948), in *There Is No Ithaca*, tr. Vyt Bakaitis, Black Thistle Press, New York, 1996, p. 41.

9 Michael Pollan, *Second Nature: A Gardener's Education* (New York: Grove Press, 2003).

10 Jonas Mekas, *Idylls of Semeniskiai*, op. cit., p. 87.

11 Jonas Mekas, *Idylls of Semeniskiai*, op. cit., p. 97.

12 Jonas Mekas, *Idylls of Semeniskiai* (1948), tr. Adolfas Mekas, Hallelujah Editions, 2007, back cover.

JAMES SHERRY is the author of 13 books of poetry and poetics, most recently *The Oligarch* (Palgrave, 2017, prose) and *Entangled Bank* (Chax Press, 2016, poetry). He is the editor of Roof Books and started the Segue Foundation in 1977 in NYC.

"I'm writing to develop an environmental model of culture that circumscribes humanism as our species already begins to adjust its position in the taxonomy of the biosphere."

William Benton
The *Idylls of Semeniškiai*

In the final poem of Jonas Mekas's *Reminiscences*, written in 1951, this passage occurs:

> Remember that time one morning we looked
> down from the lodgehouse we could feel
> every minute already lived
> sink deeper in, no longer to be torn out
> for being lived through, yet now fully felt, like
> something your own you cherish the most
> like home.[1]

It could serve as a blueprint of the process and sensibility that wrote, three years earlier—when Mekas was twenty-five—*Idylls of Semeniškiai*. On every page of these *Idylls* you can feel something like this happen. The lines move with preemptive energy, instantly beyond discourse, into what Vyt Bakaitis, who translated both books (published in 1996 under the title *There Is No Ithaca*), calls a "near ecstatic resolution."[2]

At face value these are list poems, descriptively agile, involved in saving to memory, by one of its displaced citizens, what was lost in the Soviet takeover of Lithuania at the outset of World War II. They are equally poems that delineate with remarkable purity the lines of force of their making. Description becomes, in the velocity of the language, a transmuted essence. Lithuania itself is converted to an infinite: the list can go on forever.

A poet that comes readily to mind as sharing an affinity with Mekas is Saint-John Perse. Both were forced from their homelands by the war; Perse, under his real name Alexis Leger, was General Secretary of the French Foreign Office until 1940, when the Vichy Government dismissed him for being anti-Nazi. Stylistically different (Perse, lofty and grandiose; Mekas, boyish with unrestrained ardor), both poets made the threshold between ordinary reality and art a dynamic element in their work. At times they sound like each other.

> Mekas: "You too return, along with days gone, / and flow again, my blue rivers . . ."[3]

> Perse: "Lovers who kept silent in the midst of alien crowds, you too will testify tonight in honor of the Sea."[4]

Like the sea in Perse's *Seamarks*, a Lithuania *sur sa page* comes into imperishable existence in the *Idylls*.

At twenty-five, poets are normally wary of sincerity; their work often operates within conceits of methodologies or trends. Mekas embraces it; sincerity is elevated to a transcendent position in his poems. Words shimmer at the outward edge of an unabashed purpose. Part of what makes this possible is how the line flexes its own abundance.

> The air has a dank, lingering smell of frost and raw wind,
> though gullies soon run down, drowning pastures recover,
> and along ditches and streams, as in damp ground around barns,
> marsh-marigolds start to crop up in frail yellow clusters.[5]

The momentum of listing moves the line along from one thing to another, until we get to the phrase "as in damp ground around barns," which interrupts the cadence. It holds the ear and eye in place as the syllables, like a seven-note scale, fill out the measure. It is at once artful and a condition of how the author cherishes the world he depicts.

The object of the *Idylls*—to recover loss through memory and imagination—becomes itself a finely tuned poetic mechanism.

> Then, as I lay my open hand
> against a cracked, scaley brown trunk,
> I'll feel spring, its first quiver,
> the smell of rich loam.
> So it's no longer pinebark my hand touches,
> but you, the women of my village,
> stand there on yellow sand hills . . .[6]

The tree (not there) is replaced with the women (not there) in a process that retrieves both in the lilt of their interchangeability.

These poems are not notation, but elevation. Things are preserved in Mekas's attentions, down to a radish.

> Soon it's noon, trembling and hot
> enough to choke; wilting
> whole spreads of burdock, dimming
> the gold of wild radish.[7]

The twenty-six poems that make up the *Idylls* cycle through the seasons and pastoral world of rural Lithuania with the clarity, detail, and beauty of Brueghel. Bakaitis brings to the translations not simply the credentials of an accomplished poet. He left Lithuania under circumstances similar to those of Mekas, but as a young child. It's not far-fetched to think that the intensity of these English versions has at some level to do with the finger of a four-year-old tracing, as if etched in granite, evocations of a lost past.

The foundation of memory is place. In *Time Regained*, Proust writes:

> Yes: if, owing to the work of oblivion, the returning memory can throw no bridge, form no connecting link between itself and the present minute, if it remains in the context of its own place and date, if it keeps its distance, its isolation in the hollow of a valley or upon the highest peak of a mountain summit, for this very reason it causes us suddenly to breathe a new air, an air which is new precisely because we have breathed it in the past, that purer air which the poets have vainly tried to situate in paradise and which could induce so profound a sensation of renewal only if it had been breathed before, since the true paradises are the paradises we have lost.[8]

Jonas Mekas came back from the fields of memory with stunning evidence of his.

Endnotes

1 *There Is No Ithaca*, tr. Vyt Bakaitis, Black Thistle Press, New York, 1996, p. 169.
2 op. cit., p.180
3 op. cit., p. 33: "Ninth Idyll"
4 Saint-John Perse, *Seamarks*, tr. Wallace Fowlie, Harper & Brothers, New York, 1961, p. 101
5 op. cit., p. 5: "Second Idyll"
6 op. cit., p. 13: "Fourth Idyll"
7 op. cit., p. 21: "Sixth Idyll"
8 Marcel Proust, *Time Regained*, tr. Andreas Mayor and Terrence Kilmartin, revised by D. J. Enright, vol. VI of *In Search of Lost Time*, Modern Library/Random House, 2003, p.261)

WILLIAM BENTON received his early training in music and worked as a jazz piano player before becoming a writer. His poetry has appeared in *The New Yorker*, *The Paris Review*, and other magazines. He is also the author of a number of books including *Exchanging Hats*, on the paintings of Elizabeth Bishop, and a novel, *Madly*. His most recent books are *The Mary Julia Paintings of Joan Brown* and *Backlit*. He lives in New York City.

"A six-pack (that glow), skin, / heavy overturned stones of / anguish, and the glint of loss /

on walls of polished obsidian: / this is the lamp, the zig-zag / border of its shade."

Kimberly Lyons
At the Gates of Paradise:
On the poetry of Jonas Mekas

Over the years, I've heard Jonas Mekas read his poetry at New York City's Poetry Project at St. Mark's Church and in readings in bars and galleries in Brooklyn and New York and have understood his poetry within the context of "downtown" NYC poetics. His devoted work as a filmmaker, curator of experimental film, and as a founder of the Anthology Film Archives, located in NYC's East Village; as co-founder of *Film Culture* magazine and as a writer on film for many years at the *Village Voice*, all locate his zone of activity downtown. And in that downtown way, globally.

An opportunity to investigate the whole of his poetry more closely, however, yields a revelation that Mekas's poetry is not, primarily, a poetry of transitory impressions of NYC or even of a self in relation to a landscape in flux. If a reader only read the flowers that abound in Mekas' poems and films and missed the stem and root (as in this line from a poem in the *Daybooks*: ". . . so each word burns / to the root."[1]) something essential in his poetic would be missed.

> While listening to showers
> rinsing the pink
> fresh chestnut buds,
> and to the high brook running
> downhill in rivulets,
> I missed the snow
> and whiteness.[2]

In this stanza from an untitled poem, a quintessential melancholy that may be discerned in Mekas's poems underlies the observation.

A close reading of his poetry reveals that its arc is far more expansive on all levels than a set of notations of momentary perceptions, although those modes are present. The process of poetic composition became a healing mode through which Mekas elegized loss, recorded ephemeral perceptions of beauty and rebuilt himself after the trauma of World War II.

Mekas remarks in reference to the postwar period in New York:

> During that period I was working on myself . . . and [that period] ends when I have a new family, new friends and a new set of memories. . . . I am completely somewhere else and I have escaped the war time postwar memories and depression that I had somehow managed to put myself, all those one thousand pieces, together. . . . Just at the gates of paradise. Not paradise.[3]

With his poetry, Mekas has a sustained a philosophical self that registers an internal argument between melancholy and passionate affirmation. For Mekas, poetry is a structure which contains and preserves memory and perceptions amidst flux. Paradoxes, dilemmas, psychic and historical incongruences are voiced. As film requires screening, poetry requires reading and speaking; thereby, both film and poetry are durational, ephemeral, partly art objects, partly ineffable experiences of a threshold the poet, reader and viewer may approach, but not enter.

The evolution of how Mekas's poetry brought the "thousand pieces together" may be traced starting with the early long poems *Idylls of Semeniškiai* and *Reminiscences*, which are collected in *There is No Ithaca* with English translations by Vyt Bakaitis. The later poems of *The Daybooks* and the more recent poems of *Words Apart* are of a second overlapping phase of his poetry, in which fragmentation of thought and image, notation of feeling and ellipses in time and place mirror the complex equilibrium of the young refugee. Later poems use the form to document self-reflection and momentary instances of beauty. The forms of his poems are also the result of experimentation informed by a lifetime of reading international poetry and an attentiveness to the development of mid to late twentieth century poetics. I know this in part from conversations with Jonas Mekas in which he brought forward from his extensive library books of poetry that are important to him, including works by Allen Ginsberg, Robert Kelly, and Frank Kuenstler, among the many other poetries he attends to.

Mekas notes in his autobiography *I Had Nowhere to Go* that the 26-part *Idylls of Semeniškiai* was written in Lithuanian in the winter of 1947, while he and his brother Adolfas were staying in a displaced persons camp in Kassel, Germany, following a period of forced labor, dislocation, and trauma. The extent of Mekas's WWII experience of trauma has not yet been fully described but the poems impart much. In the foreword to *There is No Ithaca*, Czesław Miłosz notes that the model for *Idylls of Semeniskiai* was the mid-eighteenth century seasonal poem written in Lithuanian by Kristijonas Donelaitis, *Metai* (1765 – 75), which pulses with the dactylic hexameter of Homer. The following excerpt is of the section "Autumn Goods" from *The Seasons*:

> The earth, welled in on all sides now, cries and complains
> Our wheels are mauling her washed-out back.
> Where before two colts could easily draw the load,
> It takes some doing to move at all now, with four horses.
> The wheel creaking on its axle turns over with heft
> And splashes great gobs of the sludge it tears off.
> Fields lie in patches, drenched and drowning everywhere now,

While the rains get at people, in splatters washing their backs.[4]

Mekas may have started to model his poem on *Metai*, but as the process of reverie and experience of poetic composition became energized, the didactic assertions, asides and moral pronouncements that occur in later stanzas of the model are left behind. In fact, there is none of that in the *Idylls*. The pulse in the *Idylls* carries the breath in an extended phrase that accumulates details. It is my intuition that it was this experience of composition that engrossed the poet, and provided a "healing" immersion in a cognition of the sensory past. In some way, this healed a rupture.

Across the span of the 26 *Idylls*, "pounding out hay swaths . . . carting oats in the heat . . . knotting rope in to fetters" and "knitting her large colorful flowers in wool" and "shaking out pitchforks of manure" draw the reader into a world. Through the course of the poem, the focus is set at a middle distance (to use a film term). As the poem progresses, a personified speaker obliquely emerges from the "we" and from the landscape represented. The lines—"I lay my open hand / against a cracked, scaly brown trunk" and "It does get tiresome, dragging up and down / wet beetbeds"—bring the reader into proximity to the things and processes described. It's not that the singular voice is preferable or necessary or an improvement over a more disembodied observation, but it seems that as Mekas developed the flexibility of consciousness that allowed experimentation, the torsion of his poem expanded. The process of even using the word "I" may have been an incremental step in a reconstruction of self.

With condensed American diction and syntax, Bakaitis's 1996 English translation of *Idylls* loosens and freshens the compact idiom of the original Lithuanian. The compound-noun phrases slightly stub the epic's flow, with words for objects just outside the perimeter of the familiar—"shrub stems" and "wing hearts" and "pinebark" and "alderscrub" and "fieldpaths" and "wheelframes" and "beetbeds" and "earth-clots" and "knife-hafts" and the poignant "pitifew"—combine to make a textured and inventive music.

From the first of the *Idylls*:

> Oh, old is the flowering clover,
> horses snorting in the summer night,
> rollers, harrows and plows scouring tillage,
> the heavy millstones rumbling,
> and women weeding the rows, their kerchiefs glimmering white.
> Old is rain gushing down shrubstems,
> cockgrouse drumming in the red summer dawn.
> Old is our talk of all this.[5]

In one breath (as in *Metai*) we are carried into a world. The specificity and mouthy English music of the terms used in the translation: "harrows," "scouring," "tillage," "millstones" concretize ineffable memory and shadow the Lithuanian idiom. The litany of actions invoked includes: "drew water," "dug yellow clay," "mowing the . . . meadows," "plows away tillage," and "roll the logs out," "roll the wagon wheels out," "drag out seed spreads and plows." These compact phrases are like tiny films. There are "horses to unshoe" and "new wheels to pin on." The long poem *Reminiscensijos* (Reminiscences) that followed the writing of the *Idylls*, is also written in a loosely epic meter and documents Mekas's thought and feeling in notations of wandering in Europe with his brother in the immediate postwar period.

> "So we pushed on / and saw people starved down to nothing / come out from under the broken brickwork, in clusters / up from the dust, in vivid stripes of concentration-camp / inmates"

> and "highways blown up / and bombcraters midfield—deep hollows / staring back black death . . ."[6]

have a Dantean, pressured rate of flow as the traumatizing memory is revived.

Whereas *Idylls* imparts a homestead scene from a youthful, close perspective, the sweep in *Reminiscences* is panoramic: "eyeing orchard slopes, trees, / and villas that hugged the hillsides" and "far out to sea / cold foam breaks from the slow-plowing / dark tugboats / " and "pour out shouting, the whole slew of us / flooding one hillside." It's as though the near hallucinatory immersion in memory that brought about the *Idylls* had dissolved—as in a film—into the long-lined energetic rush of complex phrases of *Reminiscences.* In the lines—"taking everything along, right from childhood" and "restless, with the same hunger gnawing, still / eager for each new meeting, each streetlight" and "while I keep on going, growing more and more remote"—the poet describes the process of simultaneous composition and self-observation. He splits from himself—one of many instances in Mekas's poetry of such splits—and conceives of a self of the past who views the self he becomes. The poem enacts consciousness as it presses forward, away from a time in the past (even moments ago) that the poem records.

A reader imagines that the immersion in memory at the onset of the *Idylls* was like a trance for the young poet. Rather than a state of trance producing the conditions that lead to the poem, which is one way; Mekas, instead, entered into a state of mind that the poem's conditions produced and became entranced. The poem itself produced the trance. The poet may have, after trauma, become prone to states of disassociation that then made him all the more receptive to altered states. The present could be endured with solace and return to poetry's enchanting powers.

Mekas states:

> I think I was about the age of five . . . when I got into some kind of telling to my father . . . like a sing song-ing . . . like some epics very realistic about life in the village. . . . Telling what my father did like that he went to the mill. I was so involved in it, so concentrated and so obsessed with it that I can put myself into that mood-memory whenever I return back to it. It has a . . . mood and shape . . . which later in some of my poetry cycles returns. That mood, whatever I am doing in cinema, can be retraced to what I was trying to sing out. . . . Trying to get it again. . . . I still know hundreds of songs."[7]

Calling on that mood and state of concentration may have elicited for Mekas a sense of safety, familiarity, and cohesion in the early postwar period of disorientation and chaos.

Kristin Prevallet's book *Trance Poetics* (2013) offers thinking that is useful for thinking about how the cognitive process of reception to poetry may affect and heal trauma. She elucidates a concept that physical bodies and language co-respond and change in a combined field. Prevallet writes: "Then language (a conduit to thought) has a frequency and a vibration that can shift our cellular being."[8] The possibility she asserts offers a way to think about how the writer and reader's experience of compactions of sound and cognitive complexes may (in part) heal traumatic reactions.

By the time Mekas was writing the poems collected in the *Daybooks*, he had transitioned to a new phase. The poet continues to process flashbacks. Poems now also emanate from fresh experience of the textures, sounds, and sights of NYC and various rural places. His process of composition bends away from the willed immersion in memory that produced *Idylls* and *Reminiscences*, and the poems that come after those realize and express his existential dilemma and personal contradictions; as in the *Daybooks*: "I keep pounding / on my door. / My own door!"[9]

An untitled poem written after Mekas, the young refugee, has arrived in NYC describes this juncture:

> Words come
> pouring,
> cast-off drops.
>
> Faraway
> fields, vague
> and abstract.
>
> Your own
> thoughts in scraps,
> sounding
> remote.
>
> Gateways to
> the past start
> to sway.[10]

The poet has stepped away from the "gateways" of memory and the spun thread of the epic and now sifts through "scraps."

> My life is an etching
> of letters in sand,

the words, and the ink,
this paper in your hand.

I write
with
-out any constraints.

Content and form will
settle
the field.

Memory
still
keeps bleeding.[11]

These two untitled poems above register Mekas's desire to write without restraints and to allow content to "settle" the form. A verticality of line and an intention that speech and thought shape form is of the New American Poetry; a current that he would have been exposed to since he came on the literary scene in NYC in the early 1950s. That Mekas sought fluid shape for expression is related in the later sequence "Words Apart":

I
look for
new
forms
which
would
let me,
let me
disclose

the whole
memory
of my
experience.[12]

The poems in the *Daybooks* also formulate his hope to receive and utilize details of all times and places, not just disturbed and melancholic memories and sensations. Intertwined with this desire is the poet's realization that life forms are transitory: "letters in the sand." "Memory / still keeps bleeding" is a complex phrase that condenses an array of images. Thought is in part a biological process and memory is affected in part by neurological workings of blood. Blood may not be staunched in some situations and continues to emit from openings, and so do memories and the ink of writing. The word "blood" also is used to describe the family bond. Then, there is all the bloodshed of World War II, of the Holocaust and the aftermath. With this contrapuntal, inclusive music the poet braids together memory and the present despair: "ruins" and "miracles"; yet he also registers his realization that rupture with memory and its linked feelings is impossible. In the forms of poetry, however, dialogue from past to present to future is registered that may in some way heal the frayed splits.

The poems in the *Daybooks* were generated decades after Mekas had become renowned for his tireless engagement both as filmmaker and promoter of the New American Cinema. As engaged and busy as he was, the poems state an aloneness. Introspective, yearning articulations are transcribed in a condensed, elliptical phrasing that gathers the small poems into a longer stream "… till even these / slip away in / time's stream."[13]

From *Daybooks* written in the early 1970s:

Firm up, O gods, my yearning
and let the rain of paradise
        rain on
        memory's roots.[14]

The poet asks poetry's primal protectors to bring forth creative manifestations and submits to his yearning for "scraps of my days" and "mind's / cracked, / blank / particles." What scraps come to mind? "[W]ar maps" and "accounts of concentration camps" as well as "fireballs" and "Dachau trails" and "viper's foam "and "thorns." These are lines from *Daybooks*:

Guernica
Vietnam
Katyn
Pirciupis
Kraziai

Dresden
Hiroshima
My Lai [15]

The poet asks: "is this real, / or is / it all / just a dream / you once saw." Which could be read in part as expressing the derealized mind state trauma produces even in a long aftermath. The phrase subsequently binds itself to evocations of "lush / treetops / streak / past" and "a breeze from the open car window / raking light strands of your hair " and "in the gold of sunset . . . feelings flowed / on gusts of ecstasy" and "late at night / drinking wine / think of friends / late at night" and "strawberries / a small hand / bast of linden" and "red cloverbells ... each tiny head." In fact, Mekas's string of perceptions is sequenced, unknowingly, to reflect a cognitive behavioral therapeutic technique for ameliorating Post Traumatic Stress Disorder, in which the sufferer counters disturbing flashbacks by systematically refocusing attention to the present moment's tactile, auditory, and visual sensations. Poetry transmutes the red cloverbells.

Engrossed in art and work and family, and ever exposed and involved in making, preserving seeking ineffable objects of beauty, Mekas, I believe, continued to heal from trauma as he and artist friends, such as the filmmaker Peter Kubelka, in their conversations and camaraderie came to a sense of gratitude that could generate the energy for making art:

> In the late 70s, some of what we consider are good things that we have, fragments of paradise that are still here it is our duty to . . . sustain them that they should grow . . . that is the beginning of a theme that continues through much of my thinking . . . ecstatically beautiful . . . fragments of paradise.[16]

Perhaps it is then that Mekas brought his poetry into an integration with the films and curatorial activities in the sense that the poems also came to preserve transient ephemeral passages of beauty and gestural movement. In hallowing these fragments "of paradise," he has realized that they must be treasured. Yet, paradise cannot be entered, or lived in continuously.

An encounter with Mekas's *Idylls* and *Reminiscences* was made doubly poignant in March of 2018, when the UN Refugee Agency reported that there are sixty-five million people displaced worldwide. It is also not possible to read these poems and the history they summon and not think of the European Jewish poets who wrote in Yiddish and other European languages and who were put to death in the Holocaust. I offer an incomplete list of names; an awkward insertion here, but there is no palatable place for this vastly incomplete list: Chaim Yellin, Pavel Friedman, Miklós Radnóti, Itzhak Katznelson, Mordechai Gebirtig, Karel Destovnik, Clementine Krämer, Erich Knauf, Robert Desnos.

Mekas has stated: "My country is cinema. I decided I will live in one small republic of that continent, and that republic is poetry and I support poetry and I carry the flag of poetry and I sing the anthem of poetry and poetry is my country."[17]

I think in his way, Mekas with this resolution verbalizes that he has given up on nationalistic identities and boundaries as self-defining or as the hope for the future; that he has found his allegiance to be to art and to an array of international, multi-generational, artists and to those that live for art.

I thought about the diaristic films and footage that Jonas Mekas makes in connection to his poetry. In "September 20th Rosies" which I accessed online[18], in an early version (it has since been edited) Mekas, in his mid nineties, his son Sebastian and two young fellows are at a loud, casual restaurant in Manhattan on a sunny busy day in 2017. The camera work is jumpy, swoops, arcs, and does not stay still as though restlessly trying to encompass all that is happening at once. The environment is noisy and layered. Intimate voicings underlay clashing dishes, cars honking, and peripheral conversations. Filmmaker Agnès Varda is called by cellphone and that conversation is inserted into the scene. The fellows take photos; there are frames inside of frames in Mekas's film. They all go outside and there is another movie inside the movie centered around bicycles, streets and sidewalks, and the slow rambling manner of urban leave-taking, strangers who come up to chat, and a particular kind of Manhattan restless afternoon sociability.

Throughout this film diary, the camera follows, allows, and registers, the flux and awkward moments of transition. I wondered if the pieces of a life could stay in play, if that fluid a situation furthers recovery. Conditions of unfixity provide a mobile center for movement. As Mekas commented: "Chance has its own logic. Chance may be improvisation… has stronger logic than anything you could invent. It works according to its own laws and you just do it. Just follow it. . . I'm just totally with what is happening there."[19]

In a print interview with filmmaker Jim Jarmusch, Mekas talks about how his poetics developed. Mekas cites poet Paul Celan:

> He is one of the great German-language poets. I found one of the best recent descriptions of what poetry is in this book. You can read the whole passage silently for yourself. But he ends with this: "The search for ground lights is not enough. There is the axis to be followed and '—dot dot dot—' forgotten. You must above all find lightness, buoyancy, the permanent defiance of gravity."[20]

Perhaps dislocation and its traumatic effects are countered by a receptiveness to chance. Something many refugees must come to know of. The effects of these circumstances and qualities combine in Mekas's poetry and films. Impermanence, solidity, shifting surfaces of the present and remembered solidities of the past, longing, fear of loss, and fleeting happiness. There is a continuous articulation throughout Mekas's poetry that notes the intensely-felt presence and enchantment of effluvia, flora, *agrestis* (things growing in the field) or *familiaris* (domestic, familiar); and that simultaneously anticipates loss; the condition of such things as being present, as remembered, yet going away and disintegrating. Thus paradise is not possible. Poetry, among its powers, enacts the lost by calling *what was* into being. The poet's depth of participation effects a grief work. Within the spool of the poem, the flickering now and inscribed remainders of the remembered are represented and newly experienced as an evanescent possible.

Endnotes

1 *Daybooks 1970–72*, tr. Vyt Bakaitis, Portable Press at Yo-Yo Labs, Brooklyn NY, 2003, lyric 6.

2 *Breathing Free: Poems from the Lithuanian*, ed. & tr. Vyt Bakaitis, Lithuanian Writers' Union Press, Vilnius, 2001, p. 183.

3 "The Story of Jonas Mekas" on Lousiana Channel, 2014, http://channel.louisiana.dk/video/the-story-of-jonas-mekas.(Accessed January 21, 2018).

4 Kristijonas Donelaitis, "Autumn Goods" in *Breathing Free: Poems from the Lithuanian*, op. cit., p. 49.

5 *There Is No Ithaca*, tr. Vyt Bakaitis, Black Thistle Press, New York, 1996, p. 3.

6 *There is No Ithaca*, op. cit., pp. 121 and 123.

7 "Web of Stories: Jonas Mekas," no date given, https://www.webofstories.com/about (accessed 6/3/18).

8 Kristin Prevallet, *Trance Poetics: Your Writing Mind*, Wide Reality Press, New York, 2013.

9 *Daybooks 1970–72*, op. cit., lyric 6.

10 "Words Apart" in *Words Apart and Others*, tr. Vyt Bakaitis, Rail Editions, Brooklyn NY, 2018.

11 "Some Untitled Poems" in *Words Apart and Others*, op. cit.

12 *Words Apart and Others*, op. cit.

13 *Daybooks 1970–72*, op. cit., lyric 12.

14 *Daybooks 1970–72*, op. cit., lyric 6.

15 *Daybooks 1970–72*, op. cit., lyric 43.

16 "Web of Stories: Jonas Mekas," op. cit.

17 "The Story of Jonas Mekas," op. cit.

18 "September 20th 2017 at Rosies" on http://jonasmekas.com/diary/# (accessed in January, 2018).

19 "The Story of Jonas Mekas," op. cit.

20 "Jim Jarmusch and Jonas Mekas on Film, Poetry and Trump," 2017, http://www.anothermag.com/design-living/9589/jim-jarmusch-nd-jonas-mekas-on-film-poetry-and-trump (accessed 1/25/18). Celan source unspecified.

KIMBERLY LYONS's collection of poems *Approximately Near* may be accessed online at *Metambesen.org*. Her essays on the paintings of Basil King and on the poetics of George Quasha may be accessed at *Talisman.org*. Her books of poetry include *Calcinatio* and *Capella*.

"Furthering, integuments, ineffabilities, traces, resistances, yieldings, habitats, seams, transparencies, erosions and regenerations are of interest."

Krzysztof Czyżewski
MEKASPOET

You can hardly draw a borderline between Jonas Mekas and poetry. It probably had already ceased to exist when as a boy he used to graze cows in the fields around Semeniškiai, the place that was meant to become part of the new Lithuania in the aftermath of World War I. It was not yet there on the map when he was running away from his past, leaving behind the black hole torn by war and European totalitarianisms. It was not yet there when he was returning to his childhood while learning to live in New York, with Bolex camera in hand, in constant search for the new.

Separation of life from poetry meant, in his case, being cut off from reality and eventually, exile—incomparably more dangerous than being expelled from one's native country, being a stateless wanderer, émigré, or loneliness personified in a metropolis. It meant getting out of the mouth of Leviathan, one who could cling to reality. Having experienced Hell, he bit into life, was born again to remain faithful to the poet inside.

Jonas Mekas does not compose poems; he does not set them to paper. He neither invents nor encloses words in refined formal structures. He is a poet, not a creator of poetry.

He could subscribe to Marina Tsvetaeva's statement: "Do not be afraid of the notebook with crossed out parts, nor of a blank page, but be afraid of your own wilful page."

Visitors to Jonas Mekas's room at the Anthology Film Archives will find a piece of paper on the wall with a quote from Cezanne: "Chatter about art is almost always useless." He is as economical in his words as in his life—he would not allow it to slip through his fingers. Before he utters a word, he's overwhelmed by silence. Living poetry means recovering words from silence.

Pinned there on the wall are also Gertrude Stein's words: "I am I because my little dog knows me." The poet seeks cognition and expression for himself, extrapolating himself into the space of otherness which knows him differently, thus leading him to the true self.

Also there, you will find another slip with a quote from Basho: "A poet needs to discipline himself every day." This maxim was used by Czesław Miłosz, not only in relation to his own life writing, but also to his readings of the *Idylls of Semeniškiai* as the work of "a visionary who lifts the most earthly details of reality to the highest level of intensity."

Mekaspoet inhabits the space between word and silence. The otherness determines his identity, while he himself—thanks to attention practiced in daily discipline—goes beyond the horizons marked by arbitrariness and lazy earthliness.

In an interview with Jérôme Sans, he admitted that he does not really make films, he just films: "When I film something, I don't film it because I want to create something. I do it because I want to capture the essence there, in front of me." However, the poet was there before the *filmer* was born. The camera is but an extension of the eye and all other senses of the poet.

In the center of Jonas Mekas's life stands He-Who-Watches. His is the *axis mundi* around which are deposited words and images. He is just like America from the eighth of the *Reminiscences*—immersing itself in everything that reality brings, into human fate, possession by memory and the depths of the past; "one drowning pull to wear memories down, / tear away at longings, times past, as it goes dragging / clear up into itself, to its core . . ."

He-Who-Watches makes Jonas Mekas's poetry. The writer comes too late. Only before the act of writing, in an eternal moment, words are able to return to the core itself, to the edge of silence, as in the fourth of the "Images" from *Words Apart*:

> It's just
> this image
>
> just this
> river
> -willow
> a bird
> swings
>
> just this
> burning
> sun
> in the lips
> of a stream
>
> just this.

He-Who-Watches reaches beyond memory and beyond himself. He is always farther away than the past and always closer to the other within himself. Eternally homeless, he finds his home in every moment of infatuation, in each detail of reality, if he manages to reach eternity hidden in it. He is stronger than those who never leave home—"they hate all other places."

He-Who-Watches is accompanied by the Wanderer. He left his home a long time ago, maybe with the first book he read. Since then, he has constantly been crossing new thresholds. The most, probably during the war in 1944, when together with his brother Adolfas he boarded a train bound for Vienna but was overtaken by the Germans, who sent them to a labor camp near Hamburg.

But he returns to Lithuania, as from Manhattan he returns to Brooklyn.

He is wiser than Ulysses with his experience—the loss of Ithaca is final. Real life is experienced by those who resist the sweet voices calling us "home, to which, I know, all roads have been erased." Like a dog, he can get to like many places and get attached to each. However, you cannot put down roots in each of them. The Wanderer carries inside him the wounds of the healed scars from places he was forced to leave and may yet betray.

One expelled from one's nest must push on. "We felt the pull of distance." This comes from the first of the *Reminiscences*, very Hölderlinesque in spirit. It contains the matrix of the Wanderer's route: from Flensburg to the Neckar Valley, from the North to the South, from the deadly darkness to the life-giving luminosity. The Wanderer travels from Hell, through the once proud and now shattered Center of Europe, knows killings, starvation and human degradation. Ruins tie down his feet; pain and trauma of memory stop him at railway stations that still "gave off a lingering stench of death and smoke." Lonely and miserable, he is a witness to the "deep hollows staring back black death."

The Wanderer saves the poet. He lies down to sleep in bomb craters, hungry and conscious of the human condition, unable as yet to overlook the fact that we lay there, "surviving witnesses under the first flowers of spring." He wanders on, southbound. The only answer to the questions of home and homeland—as in the eighth of the *Reminiscences*—is the act of seeing what has domesticated the surroundings: "Horizons and towns, bridges on rivers, / salt-marshes up north, windmills, / and wide-ranging autumn fields." And again: "So we pushed on." Where to? Always South, there where there is life again:

> Now here we were months later, after all that death,
> eyeing orchard slopes, trees,
> and villas that hugged the hillsides
> not believing any of it yet . . .

In the *Reminiscences*, the Wanderer leads the poet through the ruins of postwar Europe. This journey, however, may take place in the loneliness of New York or in the depression of inner life, and the South may be an empty room, a letter to friends, or a dance with a camera during a family feast. Always, however, the Wanderer helps the poet to see and positions the Beholder.

He-Who-Watches is one who left home, carrying inside the experience of the Wanderer. He has never left him, so he did not stay in places of death, in the nostalgia of escape and alienation. He stopped only at the places the Wanderer led him to, in the clearance of seeing, where poetry is born.

Mekaspoet meets us always at dawn, in daylight, our faces turned southwards. Whatever happened the night before—when the memory and the sleepless nightmare returned, when it really hurt and the wounds of consciousness opened—is checked by the poet of everyday self-discipline, purified with the power of life and subjected to spiritual transgression. Sometimes, he invites you on a journey of transformation alone, as it happens in the cycle of poems "In the Woods," in *Words Apart*, but most often we meet him lost in gazing, as in a photograph from 1948, where he sits leaning against a tree in the fields near Kassel.

In the afterword to *There Is No Ithaca*, Vyt Bakaitis recalls a fragment of the interview conducted during Jonas Mekas's return to Lithuania, in which Mekas precisely defined the place where in the autumn of 1947 for the first time since his exile, he was overcome by a sense of grief he later transformed into the *Idylls of Semeniškiai*. "Not far from the camp was a small woods and a scrawny stretch of meadow with a trickle-stream. So I'd sit there beside the stream, look at the barracks, the woods, the meadow, and dream of Semeniškiai."

Such a stream Jonas Mekas will happen to find later at various latitudes, where distance, silence, and a neighbourhood of otherness will position He-Who-Watches. Life-giving images will appear then before him, like that of aunt Kastune from the tenth *Idyll*. How does it happen that they make the poet while rescuing the exile? After all, life is not an idyll; it usually squanders these pictures, overlooks them, misplaces or simply just fails to keep them.

An image emerges from the memory: "I remember her well, our aunt Kastune." "Well" not only means "precisely," but also to reach deeper than the gloomy and destructive layer of the past. The image emerges perfect from the past, and so the eternal land of childhood continues, breeding goodness.

Aunt Kastune is far away, separated by space and time; she remains embedded in the reality purified by distance. "Distance is the soul of beauty." It is no coincidence that Miłosz cited this sentence by Simone Weil in the introduction to the American edition of the *Idylls*.

"Our immediate concerns," he wrote, "which were blinding us to the grace of ordinary things disappear and a look backward reveals them in their every minutest detail."

Images come to the poet not like an ordinary movie, in a continuum of time and space, but as if freeze-framed, shot after shot, with a space between to allow the spread of light, breath, healing of the wounds between human being and nature, between humans and objects, human and neighbour, or human and a reminiscence of the bygone. Here words have time.

The poet is a guardian of the things in-between, of what is ethereal, indeterminate, and non-literal, incompatible with the "I" itself. It's enough to use too strong a justification, *techne*'s overambitious sharpness, professionally drawn design, or an arrangement of lighting; and during the transgression of the act of seeing into the message of speech, its luminous essentiality will be erased. The act of seeing is understood here as experiencing with all your senses, including the sense of remembering. Word does not follow seeing, it is its immanent part.

The poet returns to aunt Kastune in the ritual of celebrating the crumbs of life along the paths of a deeply intimate relationship, aware that in the world dominated by a Big Number, he chooses to turn to what is small and interpersonal. He discovers fragility as the permanent material of things eternal. Words are exposed to the challenge of irrelevance and thus imprint an indelible mark on the path:

". . . we were giving everything to our Kastune." Not only peas collected in handfuls. In this space of interpersonal communion there are no limits to hospitality; there is no way to share some things and keep others to yourself. Everything is a gift and one gives another all that one owns. The luminosity of the space between does not come solely from brushing the earth with a heavenly wing, but also from the ethos of human coexistence on the earth. Here, love does not romanticize or lament; it does not shed words, but extends itself silently and infinitely.

The poet finds Aunt Kastune not by himself, nor during a nostalgic solitary journey. He always finds her with someone at his side, always in plural, within the circle of the family rites: ". . . the whole family together after chores, / with aunt Kastune there we used to sit / out under the lindens, in a circle around her …" It is surprising how rarely the singular appears in the *Idylls*. He-Who-Watches on his own will wither; he understands that the distance that pulls him is reachable only for one who does not lose sight of the other, as one in a relationship with the others in the circle.

Aunt Kastune's going away is inevitable, like a change of the seasons. So it was in childhood. For an exile, it is inevitable like the loss of home. He remains ". . . with so much to ask her," not only in the *Idylls*, but in everything that he creates. Questions will remain open. The poet, like Aunt Kastune, will not give answers. He belongs to the silence of his existence and will always return there.

All that Mekaspoet can do is to return to reality. "You don't know how much strength I need to continue running," says the Ulysess from the *I Had Nowhere To Go* diaries to Penelope/Lilly. The meaning of the author of the "Images" lies not in answering, but in immersing us in life. "Everything else," as Mekas said in his conversation with Jérôme Sans, "seemed senseless, escapist, unreal."

"'Yes, Ulysses,' said Lilly."

KRZYSTOF CZYŻEWSKI is a practitioner of ideas, writer, philosopher, culture animator, theatre director, editor, is President of the Borderland Foundation, which he co-founded in 1990, and the Director of its center "Borderland of Arts, Cultures and Nations" in northern Poland at Sejny. Together with his Borderland team, he revitalized a manor house on the Polish-Lithuanian border that for generations had belonged to the family of Czesław Miłosz and in 2011 started the International Center for Dialog there. He has also launched these dialog programs in Europe, the Caucasus, Israel, Central Asia, Indonesia, Bhutan, and USA. Since 2015 he has been a visiting professor at Rutgers University and the University of Bologna, and from his own schooldays on he has been actively involved in theatrical productions.

Among his books are poetry and essays: *The Path of the Borderland* (2001), *Line of Return* (2008), *Trust & Identity: A Handbook of Dialog* (2011), *Miłosz – Dialog – Borderland* (2013), *Miłosz. A Connective Tissue* (2014), *The Krasnogruda Bridge. A Bridge-Builder's Toolkit* (2016), and *A Small Center of the World. Notes of the Practitioner of Ideas* (2017).

In 2008 he was nominated as Ambassador of European Year of Intercultural Dialog (Brussels). He is a laureate of the Dan David Prize (2014) and the Irena Sendlerowa Prize (2015). Together with the Borderland team he is the 2018 laureate of the Princess Margriet European Award for Culture (Amsterdam).

From his essay "the ethos of an amateur":

"**The dead point must be reached by two arrows in order to revive: the first arrow is the one of belonging to nowhere, refusal; the other arrow must authenticate the first one.**"

Lina ramona Vitkauskas

Aš turiu kažkur eiti
(I have someplace to go)

For nearly thirty-eight years, I have been looking for my home.

And without question, through his films and books, as well as his poetry and visionary publications, Jonas Mekas is also looking.

For me—a forty-five year old Lithuanian-American-Canadian poet, first generation—it's a larger leap. My parents and grandparents were displaced persons from Lithuania. My father was born in Germany in a DP camp. My mother was born in Brazil after her parents fled a DP camp (Bad Salzuflen), brought to Canada—eventually she arrived in the US.

Jonas Mekas and I are generations apart. He was born the same year as my grandmother, who grew up in Kaunas and just north, Panevėžys. Mekas grew up in Semeniškiai, which is north of Panevėžys, and while he was in a DP camp in Germany, wrote hyper-sensory idylls about his childhood there.

For me, the only stories of those places that I have are from my grandparents—what little they would tell. Jonas Mekas lived through this time, and with persistent compassion his creative work explores the theme of never being able to truly return "home."

In his poetry book, *Idylls of Semeniškiai* (translated by Adolfas Mekas) Mekas takes us to a place, his home—what he remembers to be home—and he fills each idyll up: a rustic pitcher accepting fresh stream water near a blooming alder—with what John Ashbery called "unmediated pulses . . . direct as cinematography."

When Mekas wrote these idylls, he constructed stunningly lucid reminiscences of home—in spite of the dark reality of the camp environment surrounding him.

Loneliness and longing pervade these poems—with precise attention and skilled nuance. What shines through are the undeniably strong olfactory associations, for instance:

Fresh moss.
Frost and wind.
New buds.
New grass.
Alder and juniper.
Catkins and leaves.
The fresh water.
Drying meadows.
Foamy crusts.
First Coltsfoot. Swallowwort. Dandelion.
Flooded ponds.
The sun's warmth.
The last of the dirty snow.
Spring.
Drifting from the fields.
New growth.
Pine resin.
Wood.
Black soil.
White pine slats.
Earth.
Blue warm nights.
Fish and stony shallows.
All of these scents he describes transport the reader.

When he details the visions of his village—acute pastoral scenes—we see:
Wayside birch trees
Knitting needles
Crows keeping vigil
Slippery black stones
Cackling of hens
Flax, alder, potato, rye, ash berries, apples, manure, starlings.
Solitary sleighs, mouthfuls of snow
Clanking of pails, women singing, milking full cows
Oat straw, wild mustard, cabbage heads, saunas
Brushwood, mole crickets, maybugs, book-bundles
Shepherds, raspberries, honey spread on warm bread, willow fifes, wild strawberries

So many of these images: compact and vivid. So much occurring in small spaces and phrases—and yet there is an openness and freedom to these idylls, a freedom that perhaps Mekas wandered into at times so as not to face the harshest reality of DP camp and post-war poverty and chaos. These idylls are brief, but powerful: they are moments Mekas—perhaps captured between tasks and struggles within the camps—escapes to more tranquil times.

The impact of these *Idylls* to me, a once-removed daughter of Lithuania, is that I've finally begun to find my home. In reading them I am beginning to know more intimately a place I've only fleetingly visited—for even after a life-changing five-month stay, there were still things yet to learn. There were gradations and secrets of the land to listen to, absorb.

In a 2017 interview with Jim Jarmusch for *AnOther* magazine, Mekas said of poetry written in other languages: "When you don't know the language and you listen, and you seem to understand, but you get completely something else . . . you get some of the same spirit, there is something that remains." With the *Idylls*, the reader has the purest translation—by Mekas's own flesh and blood—and yet there is still an exquisite, embedded code between the lines—like sowed fields, unknown seeds still buried.

I've found that even though I have personally seen the fields of Lithuania of which Mekas waxes nostalgic—and because of these images, I feel closer to my homeland—there is still such a confidential aspect to these poems: seasonal vignettes from Mekas's own village. Of course, I will perhaps never see Semeniškiai the way Mekas did after a return to his village—he documented this on film—he also realized this. The passage of time, in fact, had either altered or enhanced his memories and experiences. Mekas wrote, "I had no place to go," and in response I say: now we have someplace to go. Both of us, however, still children of our homeland at ages ninety-four and forty-five, are making our way, just beginning or rounding the bend, finally coming home.

LINA RAMONA VITKAUSKAS was born in 1973 to wolves of Lithuanian, Canadian, and Brazilian descent. As an infant, she roamed the dark forests of the world. Most recently, she was the voice of George Maciunas's mother in Jeffrey Perkins's documentary *George,* and created a series of cinepoems with visual artist Tess Cortes (based on Vitkauskas's book *White Stockings* (White Hole Press, 2016) about mythical, Baltic female snipers). Lina has written several poetry books about first-generation identity crisis, and has expressed ekphrastically her respect for directors Antonioni, Frankenheimer, and Bergman in her collection *A Neon Tryst* (Shearsman Books, 2013). She was selected by Eleni Sikelianos for the Henry Miller Memorial Library Ping Pong Journal Award, and by Brenda Hillman for The Poetry Center of Chicago's Juried Reading Award. Publications: *Vilnius Review, Berfrois, Dusie* (Canada), *Resist Much, Obey Little* (Spuyten Duyvil), *Rain Taxi, VIDA, The Conversant,*

VLAK (ed. Louis Armand, Edmund Berrigan), and many others. Website: linaramona.com.

"I must save the planet from destruction by becoming my true self: a telepathic-shape-shifter-super-heroine!"

Brenda Iijima

An Archive of Fleeting Pathos,
Daybooks 1970–72

Jonas's oeuvre translates momentary impressions into iconic remembrance. Always the lightest, gossamer touch is enabled, then attuned by a reverence for slippage and loss. Fleeting emotions and images rush into focus and dissipate. The contingencies of history flow as daydream, as nightmare hallucination, as abject reality, as quotidian hint; chronology in the form of a trace. Details are dynamic and vital. Subtle shifts of attention within an intimacy of contemplation are interrupted by herculean and brutal circumstances. An archive of pathos accrues. All of Jonas's films and writing participate in these qualities. I'd like to focus on *Daybooks 1970–72*, published in 2003 by my then fledgling press, Portable Press at Yo-Yo Labs.

Publishing *Daybooks* was an incredible gift of confidence for me as a young poet and an inexperienced publisher. Jonas didn't blink an eye when I approached him and solicited work—he offered two luminous manuscripts to choose from. A portal of energy had opened up. An unpublished manuscript is an unlegislated force field, and to have the chance to consider two works side by side was a generative experience that stimulated my desire to take very seriously the role of poet-publisher and consider the cultural and political meanings that are developed by bringing forth a printed document into a social space. My first approach was going to be an interview but then, somehow, I switched gears and thought, no, a book—that's what needs to happen. At the time, Jonas had only one book of his poetry published in English translation, but the same translator also had done *Daybooks,* so that now Vyt Bakaitis, Jonas's good friend and soulful advocate of his work, is forever linked to the book. His exquisite evocations in English of Jonas's lyrical cascades bind together their Lithuanian cultural heritage and experience of immigration to the United States. *Daybooks* consists of poems interspersed with still frames from Jonas's films and also newspaper clippings.

Daybooks is a surprisingly compact volume considering that it chronicles a few years of the life and times of a downtown New York filmmaker-poet who is as socially connective as Jonas is. Although spare in terms of word count, the book is anything but minimalist. Lines have gravitational pull. Phrasing is concise because the evocative quality of each utterance opens up space manifoldly, a shorthand for effulgent gesture. Thoughts are so direct as to lay bare affective states. Colloquial, down-to-earth awareness is delivered in real-time. "A true account of the actual is the rarest poetry, for common sense always takes a hasty and superficial view."[1]

The cinematic quality of *Daybooks* is evoked by the pacing of short fragments that descend down the page. The eye roves, rests, focuses. And at the same time the sound of language asserts itself, momentarily displacing the primacy of sight, into an accumulation that involves simultaneity and doubling. Language conjures image, image conjures language, conjures sound. Sight and sound enable each other.

> 22.
> Here's
> a poem for
>   you.
>
> Three ducklings
> squatting
> on ice.
> Milky down,
> marsh marigold feet,

dream eyes,

December
down.

Regenerative feedback occurs when sensory signals are transmuted all the while resisting vertiginous spirals away from context, contact, camaraderie. Connections at multiple points. Variance. Envelopment. An invitation to come closer to the phenomenon.

Jonas relates the process he engages when making film diaries and diaries made up of language:

> Since 1950 I have been keeping a film diary. I have been walking around with my Bolex and reacting to the immediate reality: situations, friends, New York, seasons of the year. On some days I shot ten frames, on others ten seconds, still on others ten minutes. Or I shot nothing. When one writes diaries, it's a retrospective process: you sit down, you look back at your day, and you write it all down. To keep a film (camera) diary, is to react (with your camera) immediately, now, this instant: either you get it now, or you don't get it at all.[2]

Yet the words on the page do not always feel retrospective, interspersed are reminiscences, but for the most part the utterances feel in time: a "now" that is briefly held in suspension. Jonas toggles between spontaneity and contemplation throughout his oeuvre. This book balances these tendencies. There is also no attempt to be conclusive. We don't know what day each entry is logged. There are seventy-six entries recorded in the space of the few years.

29.
ragged snow patches
    glinting

blood-tipped wind lashing
walk and
      your veins
   grow
ecstatic

feel it
  swing and flutter
        childhood

sunlight classics

The writer Nathalie Sarraute has defined her work as the "movements that are hidden under the commonplace, harmless instances of our everyday lives."[3] Her statement relates to Jonas's modality of out-stretch, extending toward the beacons of identification, the charisma of presence. Atmosphere casts a spell and is also the air we breathe for sustenance. We move in and out of circles of affinity, in and out of unknown depths of focus. Myriad presences intersecting, relating. Days are flickering trajectories that connect space and time, hesitate between light and dark. The sun's rays create a spectrum of color and light that is absorbed by skin, blood, bone—conducts hormonal symmetries, asymmetries, calibrations. Always within an ecological whole—an orb spinning in vast unfathomable space is where we are in the poem.

27.
Cold,

numb,
coppered
autumn
fingers

dream of
      bare
buds turning
      green.

These poems are oriented by ecological information. Human existence is an ecological condition. Somatic sensations ripple through syntax.

Humanity is the subject of these poems, self-relating socially within historical contingency. Firmly planted in a human ontological narrative the poems are the residual moisture of a day. To be born on planet Earth in 1922, within iterations of globalized conflict. Displaced from home, from familiar ecosystem. Originating in a pastoral milieu—life on a farm. Forced into conflicted and violent conflagrations as destruction cancels almost everything known, held dear, recognizable. Differentiating the light of the sun from the blast of gunfire, tank fire, bombs—reclaiming the light holistically. Humans—humanity: a symbiotic trajectory of mineral and energy, simultaneously perplexingly estranged from nature ("nature") and also always nature's imprint. War's implicit goal is to eradicate holism, to blast interrelations. Residual delineations of spirit amidst the rubble that has survived conflict; semblances of the past that continue to glow. In these poems is a refusal to distance oneself from historical and personal histories but somehow not at odds with Etel Adnan's powerful statement: "I distance myself from my distance."[4] There is a reckoning regarding how history processes and records displacements in both Etel and Jonas's lyrics. Exile is a movement trajecting through

Jonas's entire biographical record. Dramatic embodiment of a state of loss is paradoxical and real. Cleaving to remnants of what one was forcibly detached from is a way to regain a sense of stability.

30.
I looked back,
   and a pillar
      of salt

crashed
   my childhood
windows

in on Kaziuk's
toy horses made of clay.

I'm Lot,
walking
now
beside my young daughter,

her small hand
showing me
the way . . .

Resplendence for Mekas isn't reliant on material possession, capitalist drives of desire, identification with power. His is an ontology that presides in shimmering immediacy and indeterminacy constantly concerned with the self's proximity to beloved communities. To locate communality within catastrophic consequence and the brutal force of power, again and again. Loneliness and despair saturate the psyche, the words, the sequences of affective experience. The longing borders on sentimentality, but this seems obviously necessary in a time and space that devalues tenderness, wistfulness, and reminiscence. A comment that Jonas made about Marie Menken's films also relates intimately to his poems: "The realist sees only the front of a building, the outlines, a street, a tree. Marie Menken sees in them the motion of time and eye. She sees the motion of heart in a tree. [. . .] A rain that she sees, a tender rain, becomes the memory of all rains she ever saw; a garden she sees becomes the memory of all gardens, all color, all perfume, all midsummer and sun."[5] The daily entries gather energy around symbols of struggle as proof of resistance.

61.
roadside icon
hilltop cross
heart of a bell

the field rye
the linden limb
the forest moss

city gates
dusty footpath
blood duct

viper's foam.

Daybooks opens upon a rain-soaked metropolis, hushed by precipitation. The clamor of the city is fractionalized into tiny details of color and motion.

I sit
    drink my beer

look out the window

it's raining

newspaper on head
    a man
        runs by

woman
a green raincoat

red street
    crossings

sidewalk
    weaving
    wet

I sit
    drink my beer
look out the window

A moment in time is framed by a quotidian instance of recognition. The poet, from his room, peers out the window, sips beer, senses the rain, notices a man running along the street, protecting his head with a newspaper, a woman wearing a green raincoat punctuated by a red street crossing light—a moment that is linked to history by a diaphanous chain of events. Incidental, casual, peripheral, proximal. Banal if not for the calibrated conviction that every moment is full of scintillating detail and potential for intimate feeling. To take the blinders off. To participate in wonder. As if taking a directive from poet Joan Murray and a canny interplay of past, future, and present:

If, here in the city, lights glare from various source,
Look out of your window, thin faced man.
Three portent cities repeat the pattern and the course
That history ran.[6]

Reality—the way reality flickers in and out of focus potentially induces a state of transfixing wonder. Joan Murray's poem dates back to 1947. There is the slightest chance that Jonas read her untitled poem. Variations of days, of lives, and recollections thereof. Observational affinities in time. Thanks to Farnoosh Fathi, editor of Murray's posthumous collection, her poem upsurges once again, in a new publication and intersects here, with Jonas's crystal-clear cognizance. It thrills me to unite these poem-fragments and see the sparks fly. Consider "from various source," and now consider "red street/crossing"—spatial cues that relate to psychic calibration as time accretes affinities of apperception.

Simplicity of statement. A memo that lists frustrations, sorrows, joys, and existential fear. Notations of history impacting the spirit. The reader is left to supply content when it seems missing in vast categories of thought and feeling.

24.
life's pits
life's leftovers
life's meadows
death's props

Atrocities take a lifetime to process—and are never truly resolved. Poems reveal a coping mechanism and offer momentary relief.

28.
I learned my geography
from war
maps.

Human anatomy
I came to grasp
from
accounts of
concentration camps.

Dispersed among the poems are three jarring images taken from newspaper clippings as well as several stills from Jonas's films. The photographs punctuate, resettle, and complicate adjacent language, thus breaking with complacency. Each photo brings with it a set of valences and contextual orientations, shifting how we think about the documentation of memory and event. Poems give a deceptive sense of not being of a moment, or in a moment. On viewing these images, we come to realize they are re-photographed photos, that they have a primary relation elsewhere, and bringing the images into this book inserts them in a different timeline. Juxtaposed, the photos and the poems comment on time, acting as a reminder of the less than easy or fluid somatic experience of navigating a chronology of events and affective realities. The photos defy sequential telling and retelling. The semantic content of the photos adjusts the focus of the poems and vice versa. They are insurgent portals into the psychic space of the social and amplify an inventory of historical events that are at once tangential and central. The poems float upon surface reality, whereas the images puncture that reality with stark hyper-perception, wresting at gestures of sublimation and denial—the images flash up like epiphanies of negative space-time. A fourth dimension is suddenly made visible. Revelations more intense and daunting than fantasies are activated; machinations of violence—visible and invisible—to define the polity.

48.
Sing in
calm
    I no longer can.

In deep
anguish
I can't write down

I follow
the death
of my own
irresponsible
generation.

The first of the newspaper images shows three soldiers crowded around a man wearing only a loincloth who looks to be unconscious; his arms are twisted behind his back; he is being held down by a soldier while a soldier-accomplice looks on as a third soldier has his boot poised above the head of the man they are menacing. The caption to the photo states: "PRISONER: South Vietnamese soldier kicks suspected Viet Cong member who was captured near Xumchung. The man was among thirteen guerrilla suspects taken in recent action." The violence the photo reveals is a fractionalized moment in a history that can never be fully conveyed or disclosed. The photo, cut out of a larger context, brings a realization of how quickly images circulate and are then forgotten—or abandoned—relegated to a neglected timeline. Underscoring how much we are unaware of, how much passes outside of conscience, the image conjures a nexus moment of identification in a blurred continuum of antagonisms and resolutions.

As I consider the role of the images in Jonas's *Daybooks*, I keep in mind Rosalind E. Krauss's discussions in her book, *The Optical Unconscious* (1994). I'm interested in "the gesture that comes from outside the subject" that she writes about in relationship to "the one who gives 'I' its (existential) meaning in the act of speaking," which structural linguists call the "subject of enunciation."[7] And I contemplate also Lacan's notion of extimacy as it applies to an intimate identification with a subject "outside" or of the outside, external world; "what is closer to us but nevertheless exterior to us."[8] Jonas, as curator of the images selected for inclusion in his book of poems—pointedly titled *Daybooks*—is shifting his agency from intimate encounter to a more global social perspective, but also simultaneously re-inscribing the intimacy of contact he has engendered with these images. By choosing to include particular images out of a plethora of images available and those he has collected over his lifetime he is amplifying his connection to them. The visual explicitness of these photos butts up against the softer focus and gentle tone of the poetry herein.

Experience is simultaneously fragmentary and holistic. Isolated and repositioned in a different setting and a different time frame, this photo of a not-so-distant war haunts the present. The image is startling and deeply upsetting. A documentation of a heinous crime, rendered in black and white pixels that have already faded before the image is reproduced in a book of poems. The photo in its first iteration was widely circulated through Associated Press channels. We are implicated, as voyeurs and as members of a colonial occupier that has waged a campaign that is beyond the scope of comprehension because of the layers of propaganda and the distance from us at which it occurred—and yet, the pain is in front of us, flickers as headline, discarded footage in history's dustbin. The newspaper clipping states the date is October 23–24, 1965. Jonas has held onto the image for thirty-eight years before it becomes integrated into the *Daybooks*. How long does our gaze rest on the photo? Can we endure looking at the photo? Alterity is a result of national campaigns of violence.

I remember discussing with Jonas how the clippings would be arranged in the book from the thick envelope of images he wanted to include. He had untold folders of images he collected at Anthology Film Archives, and at his home. We settled on fewer images than he first conceived. This gave the poems, newspaper clippings, and stills a greater impact in relation to each other as varied modes of media and mediation—a starkness and an immediacy of presence. A film still of his elderly mother sitting on a little wooden bench in a wooded thicket, dappled sunlight cascading around her—she looks directly at the camera, her posture relaxed. One frame directly above in the same sequence has an image of a clover blossom, close up, slightly blurred, possibly filmed at the same setting as Jonas's mother who is enveloped by afternoon light. The underbrush takes on heightened significance—lushness and aliveness beckons. Experiential data is suffused with emotional energy. A confluence of feelings floods the book.

56.
Full light of
paradise
still shines
behind your
silk
lashes.

Endnotes

1 Henry David Thoreau, *A Week on the Concord and Merrimack Rivers*, Boston: James R. Osgood and Company, 1873, p. 344.

2 http://www.closeupfilmcentre.com/film_programmes/2016/close-up-on-jonas-mekas/walden

3 https://www.ndbooks.com/author/nathalie-sarraute/

4 Etel Adnan, *To Look at the sea is to become what one is*, "XVIII", New York: Nightboat Books, 2014. p.201,

5 http://hcl.harvard.edu/hfa/films/2009janfeb/menken.html

6 Joan Murray, *Drafts, Fragments, and Poems: The Complete Poetry*, New York Review of Books Poets, 2018, p.3.

7 Rosalind E. Krauss, *The Optical Unconscious*, MIT Press, 1994, p 23.

8 David Pavón-Cuéllar quoting Jacques Lacan, http://www.academia.edu/4374516/Eximacy

BRENDA IIJIMA's involvements occur at the intersections and mutations of poetry, research movement, animal studies, ecological sociology and submerged histories. She is the author of seven full-length collections of poetry and numerous chapbooks and artist's books. Her most recent book, *Remembering Animals* was published by Nightboat Books in 2016. She is also the editor of *the eco language reader* (Nightboat Books and PP@YYL). She is the founding and current editor of Portable Press at Yo-Yo Labs, located in Brooklyn, NY (http://yoyolabs.com/).

"The collective death of the majority of plants and animals on planet Earth is a mass extinction happening before our human-animal eyes, happening because of human destruction of habitats (in the form of mining, infrastructure development, farming, oil and gas production, toxification and overpopulation of humans)."

Yuko Otomo

The *Daybooks* of Jonas Mekas

An exile.

There are two ways of being "exiled." One is to self-exile with one's will. The other is to be in forced exile. "Self-exiling" is like planting your life in different soil knowingly. You choose it for whatever reason you have. In the case of "forced exile," you have no choice. You are thrown into the unknown without consent or knowledge of the possibilities or impossibilities of the moment or the future. Either way, the life of an exile is filled with uncertainties & difficulties caused by unfamiliar circumstances. An exile carries the *melancholy* of being a stranger no matter.

Jonas had no choice. He had to follow the path set by fate. Forcefully being ripped from his origin, moving through moment to moment, from place to place, he had no other choice but to survive to live or live to survive. The humble weight of this book, full of immeasurable sadness, yearnings, anger, despair, & hope is staggering. I need to be alone to read it in silence. It is heartbreakingly personal. The cruel fragility of history weaves itself through life, then & now. Life passed & life being lived at this moment criss-cross. He talks of being an exile, a refugee, an estranged poet of moving images & words, a father of a small daughter & a man of 58 years of age. He carries unfathomable haunting memories inside him wherever he goes. He has no choice. He lives them & they live him. Memories have become the flesh & bones of his being. They keep living *in* him, *through* him, & *as* him. His voice is clear, simple, & direct. It is radiant, quiet, & powerful. It is one long poem. It is a monologue.

I sit

drink my beer

look out the window

"I" in poetry is a strange thing. "I" can be strictly & definitely personal, excluding all other "non-I's" from the voice. At the same time, the same "I" can be an indefinite "I" that invites us all to be the person who is talking. Jonas's "I" speaks in both voices, in definite & indefinite tones, sharing thought & memories. He talks to himself. It is like singing a lullaby to himself. I listen to his voice as if it were our *shared* voice & its echo.

It is Jonas who is drinking beer & looking out the widow. Broadway is wet & busy. He is alone in his own meditation. He is talking of what he sees on the sidewalk as I overlap myself with his "I." He does not brush me off or welcome me. He just lets me be his "I" without asking me any questions. So I become him.

So now "I" am drinking beer looking out his window. Looking down on the sidewalk where human lives bustle, we see the same sidewalk alone together.

Rain(ing).

Light or heavy, it is a word to describe a clear liquidity in a constant motion of falling. When rain gets frozen on the ground, it becomes ice. When rain gets frozen way above us, it becomes snow. A snow covered sidewalk soon needs to be plowed. Once warmed up, it melts, becoming its liquified self, again. Many forms of metamorphosis of a simple liquidity of rain provide us different backdrops for life. It rains constantly in *Daybooks.* Tears falling from the sky never stop. A phenomenal liquidity shared by both tears & rain is dreamlike in its fragility here. How strange to realize that rain has no taste but tears do! Sweet or bitter, tears do have a taste.

I am glad this book is called *Daybooks*, not *Nightbooks*. If it were *Nightbooks*, I would not be able to hold it in my hands as I am doing now. What different poetic effects these two nouns hold! Night & Day. Day & Night. Because it is "Day" books, I can go on leafing through dark, at times, extraordinarily bright & beautiful memories of his. The noun "Day" gives me an affirmation to trust my own sense of the Joy of Life. Jonas is extraordinarily sensitive to every slight shift of moisture & airflow wherever he is. He remembers what he saw, heard, & witnessed physically & metaphysically with such clarity. His memories keep talking to him. I go through every delicate emotional shift of the moment with him.

good to sing
sad to cry
tears flow in
jug of joy

Wordless.

When you are ripped out of the origin of who & what you are, you don't just feel alienated from the new reality but fall into a pit of "wordless-ness," so to speak. It is as if you are thrown into some dark, unfamiliar & unknown space where the collapse of your own language system starts to take place. It is not that there is the void of words. No. Ironically, words are around you, more than ever. Plenty of them. But the words around you are not yours. Singularly or collectively, *they* are not speaking *your* words. You have *your* words: *your* mother tongue. Now, your language is like a tree forced to grow secretly inside you as no one sees it or hears it. You are keenly aware of the new circumstances. Maybe, too sensitive to them. A threatening cacophony of unknown words occupies the world of uncertainty you now live in. You hear different sounds & wonder over different meanings of words. In this new wordless-ness, you keep pounding your own door.

Take pity on me, gods.
Firm up, O gods, my yearning
and let the rain of paradise
        rain on
        memory's roots.

Like impressions burnt & chiseled on photo or film negatives, memories, words, & landscapes of his lost world never go away. He cannot brush them off. He does not want to. They are the irreplacable, vivid evidence that tells him of who & what he is. Where does he come from? What constitutes his being? Without memories, he will be in a partial void, losing the sense of identity that confirms his being. Memories live in him. They live as if to compensate for what has been taken away from him. They are here as long as he lives. As he remembers, he rains tears for his pain & the pain of others. All the unanswered questions of life fill his mind & heart. What a cruel thing to have memories as the lifeline to your own assaulted & demoralized reality! You have no other way but to seek answers through living with memories in order to grab the content of what happened fully & to understand the why & how of your own history.

by thin
blood threads

my language
still clings to

childhood
blue

pale
sunbleached
boards
cracking

My language. My mother tongue. The language I learned to read & write as a child. The language I spoke as a child. The language I heard others speak. The language that speaks of me when I want to say something fluently & naturally. The language that flows like water. But now I speak a language that is not mine. It does not flow as I wish it to. Am I saying it correctly? Am I hearing it right? Am I understanding it for what it actually means? Tossed back & forth over doubts & uncertainty, the language I speak & hear now becomes my new self.

An intricately complex uncertainty makes him tremble slightly, whenever he tries to say what is on his mind. Something is somewhat awkward. Nothing echoes naturally. He cries for himself & others who share the pain of being cut off from home & its language.

Where do I belong?

But I go on living
in a daze,
a bit remote,
like a misfit. . . .

Some kind of born
dissident;
worse yet,

an anarchist!

Yes, you *do* need an exclamation mark here! A misfit. A born dissident. An anarchist! With a book of poems in his pocket, he walks in the rain. Lost inside himself, he walks, questioning civilization & history as his memories, pastoral & dreamlike, cruel & despairing, keep haunting him.

Memories of childhood. Memories of a home he was forced to leave. Home where potatoes blossomed white, birch trees stood soundly & strongly, pastures & fields opened up softly to the gentle horizon. Home where flowers bloomed in colors & fragrances with bees busily buzzing around them. Home where his family & culture come from. Home where his father was shoved against a wall & he lay face to the ground. Home he had to escape from. Home where he was driven out. Home where he looked back. Home he would never forget. Home he does not want to forget. Home where his mother tongue speaks what is on his mind. Home that keeps living inside him as "HE."

Why all these tragedies? Why all these tears? Why all these wasted & assaulted histories? Why so much violence: a dark energy & a psyche of the monstrosity of humanity? Why so much pain? Why? Why? Why? An unsolvable "nowhere to go" sense of guilt of those who have survived haunts him.

sad as
rain
falling

He walks feeling the air. He is delicately aware of who he is now & then. Who was I? What was I thinking? Who am I? What am I thinking? Thoughts & feelings mix their colors & music, weaving them into some intangible thread. What he thinks & how he feels overlap. Then, rain. More rain, again. More rain from the sky & his & others' tears. From memories.

Although he was not a child but a young adult when he left home forever, whenever I think of Jonas's experience, I cannot stop thinking of the film *Ivan's Childhood* by Andrei Tarkovsky. Human brutality & atrocity seen by the innocent eyes of a child: a child who was pulled into the whirlpool of darkness & cruelty without ever wanting or dreaming to be part of it. The child's eyes see everything with his wide open consciousness.

> I learned my geography
> from war
> maps.
>
> Human anatomy
> I came to grasp
> from
> accounts of
> concentration camps.

I have never "experienced" such an accurate & powerful expression of an indictment on human darkness. I do not "read" these words in the ordinary sense of reading a poem. I take them in, get beaten & shaken by them. Totally. It is as if his words come directly from his soul to be placed on the table of our moral consciousness. How painful & impossible it is to imagine him fleeing, looking back at his home—like Lot! A pillar of salt. Fear & awe. Yes, tears have a taste of salt, bitter or sweet.

As I read his *Daybooks*, *other* Jonases all over the world are experiencing similar circumstances, trying to escape from their own birthplaces to become exiles as he did. How desperately strange & how unacceptably grotesque it is to see/hear the same story again & again like a recurring nightmare! As I breathe, violence never stops, & atrocities keep taking place. Where are we? Where are we going? What are we? Time passes. In the midst of haunting memories, his young daughter's small hands show him the way.

More rain. More tears. & more rain.

Rain melts
the grieving.

Why do we cry when pain becomes intolerable? Why do we shed tears? How does pain induce tears? Where do tears come from? From the heart? From the soul? Or is it just a corporeal phenomenon? What constitutes tears? How do emotions & the physicality of our beings connect to create a clear liquidity we call tears? Why do tears drip or pour out of our bodies? Why are they clear & have no color? Why do they have a salty taste? Strangely, it seems that nothing can dissolve the unbearable pain at the end but tears. They *wash* the utmost pains away literally with their liquidity.

After melting the grieving with rain, the sun shows up to brighten the world. How the world shifts itself toward its brilliant inherited goodness according to the light given! Everything is brighter & more alive when the sun is out, even the dark memories.

sun
sidewalk

green dress
tree
green meadow
grass

Sunlight crosses tears. Tears become sunlight. The transparent clarity of tears invites the translucent clarity of light. In bustling city sidewalks & noisy traffic, memories of gently swaying birch trees & red maples come back to him vividly. Paradise & Hell, past & present, pastoral & urban, all crisscross with fragile intricacy upon life & death. All tremble together in an autumn wind as he walks on the thistle-blooming path of his memories. Is it real, or is it a dream? Walking, his mind wanders.

I go
thinking of
death and
my friends.

He trembles in the meadow of a remembrance. He has no choice. He walks on wet nameless gravel in rain as a "grown" man. He walks thinking of destiny in general. What is it? Who gives it to whom? What really happened? Why did it happen? What is really happening? The pain & anger he feels are beyond words. Here, again, he is wordless.

Sing in
calm
    I no longer can.

In deep
anguish

I can't write down . . .

Rawness of the darkness he experienced is so intense that he dares to stare at it directly. An indescribable sense of regret comes back to him, & he does not know how to reconcile with it to calm his heart. He cannot forget. Memories do not want to be forgotten. Memories do not leave him alone. Memories keep speaking to him in his aloneness despite him. Being an exile, he lives the life of a survivor. Everything betrays him. Even his own generation. Most of all words & language betray him. What are you to do when language betrays you? Keep silent? Keep trying to say something that does not deliver your soul's message smoothly? So, he writes in his language lost & found. He writes for himself & for those who died. With the language of his lost & found childhood, he writes something that he cannot write in words.

Rain keeps falling on him wherever he goes. On the streets or in a field of memories, a rose-scented melancholy cradles a sense of the infinite, such as the sky inside him. In the vast landscape of the past & the present, he feels at home being a Romantic in exile. What else can he be but a Romantic after all those unimaginable events he has experienced? So, he listens to Mozart, thinking, observing blue flowers in a vase.

Oh: let it rain on
the parched, scorched lips words have,
on grammar.

More rain . . .

then come pouring, raining down,
on the skyline

and on my soul.

& more rain.

He sheds tears. The sky that witnessed everything also sheds tears. He is only a small voice in the scarred & unscarred vast landscape of uncountable memories. Millions & millions of various voices of sadness fall from the sky, together or alone & no one can stop them.

tentative
rain falling

life's
bitterness

& more rains. But, then . . .

sun,
O sun . . .

He kneels down. He cries for the sun with his hand to his face.

I survied.
You survived.
He & she, they survived.

We survived it all!

Others, he or she,
could not . . .

Did not . . .

Ellipsis.

Three small dots carry what the words cannot say. Three small dots of "nothing-ness" open the door of unstoppable emotions that have no shape, form, or voice. Thoughts & memories, bitter & sweet, tremble together embracing each other in silence. All the unanswerable questions & answers rise & sink again. They come & go like waves. Oh, fate! Oh, destiny! Oh, humanity! Oh, darkness & light! Answer me . . . answer my questions . . . all my questions . . .

As a survivor, he bears the extraordinarily heavy weight of something unsolvable on his heart & soul. Voices & images of those who did not survive haunt him as fate shows the hub of Paradise in messy fragments here & there. How cruelly sad it is that those who did not survive can only live on in a survivor's memory. Without being remembered by someone who is alive, they will be totally gone, erased from history, unrecognized. Memories, sweet & bitter, haunt him. The more haunted, the more he remembers. The more he remembers, the more he cherishes life. The more he remembers what happened & what did not happen, the more an intricate & breakable delicacy of life awakens him. Finally, light. Now light & dark walk hand in hand.

I go on no hope,
yet remain
an idealist . . .

still
believing
in
miracles.

A still life like the truth of life reflects itself on fruit, bread, & milk in his room. Life & death for nothing. Nothing for nothing. All is like a dream. He walks the city street, dazed, thousands of miles away from his home & his childhood memories, still believing that Paradise is not totally lost. Not yet. Oh, miracles! His heart is open for them no matter what. He keeps walking the autumn sidewalk, America, asking both non-exiles & exiles the same question.

> Have you ever walked
> alone,
> down strange city streets,
>
> knowing you were
> alone like this
> with autumn,
> your coat
> soaked through,
>
> all alone
> with your
> Lithuanian words for
>
> autumn, wet sidewalk,
> the wind, the dampness,
> *All Quiet on the Western*
> *Front . . .*

All was quiet & nothing was new on the Western Front. In sepia-colored multiple stills of the moving images of his life, a poet praises the beauty of life in silence, holding a small rose gently between his fingers. He meditates alone on the timelessness of its color, thorns, delicious scent, & the clear blood inside. Everything is breathing every moment. Day to night to day to night to day, dislocated & exiled, together with roses & their miraculous gentle fragility, he is in eternity breathing his & others' memories of now & then. He speaks to himself in his mother tongue, not lost, but soundly alive inside him. The bitterness & sweetness of life. Finally, he sees both equally.

Soon winter will come & spring will follow. Memories of pastoral beauty lost & found in his life will blossom inside him again as he breathes the city air. I close the book as I close my eyes.

YUKO OTOMO is of Japanese origin. A visual artist and a bilingual (Japanese and English) writer, she writes poetry, haiku, art criticism, and essays. Her publications include *Garden: Selected Haiku* (Beehive Press), *Fragile* (Sisyphus Press); and *Small Poems, The Hand of The Poet, STUDY & Other Poems on Art* (all from Ugly Duckling Presse), as well as *Elements* (the Feral Press), *KOAN* (newferalpress) and *FROZEN HEATWAVE,* a collaborative linked-poems project with Steve Dalachinsky (Luna Bisonte Prods). She regularly writes for a collective critical writing forum www.Arteidolia.com.

"**sparrows & mourning doves not visiting our kitchen window sill anymore**"

Basil King
Dear Vyt,

Just in time before the New Year I finished Jonas's diary, *I Had Nowhere to Go*. The most compelling thing that articulates his survival in slavery and then in the DP camps before he arrives with his brother in New York City is that he insists on having books. Books, hundreds of books. I don't know how he did it but there again catch him if you can. He never lets the left hand know what the right hand is doing. Jonas is a man of mystery.

Pause

Jonas and his brother Adolfas arrive in New York City October 29, 1949, take one look at the city and decide to forfeit their jobs in Chicago and remain in New York. They move to Williamsburg, Brooklyn and for years they work menial low paying jobs.

Pause

Jonas does what the lonely do and that is he creates and in his case not fantasies or daydreams, he keeps a diary, he writes poems that walk the reader through what disturbs him, and that keeps him balanced. In his diaries he makes acute observations of the political situation and his fellow inmates. In the factory and the DP camps he remains true to his homeland. He remembers his mother, the landscape, and is never sentimental about his childhood, the smell of hay, days in the fields. The interactions of people. He uses his intelligence and his erudition to step out of a situation that could render him impotent. He never overcrowds his poetry with what was taken away from him he discriminates and internalizes history.

Pause

Years ago Baraka (LeRoi Jones) received a letter written in Japanese, Roi asked Matsumi (Mike) Kanemitsu to read it to us.

I'd been to Japanese movies. But this was the first I'd heard a letter read aloud in Japanese. The letter was from a Japanese poet. He loved *Yugen*, a magazine that Baraka and Hettie Jones published. He complimented my drawing for the cover and the contents in the magazine. It was a hoot!

I've heard Yuko Otomo read her "Anonymous Landscape" ... it is in 200 parts fragmental poems on "anonymity" two times. She reads the poem in English. I was so taken with the poem the first time I heard her read I was certain she was reading in Japanese and that I understood the Japanese. When she finished there was much applause. Martha said, "you're not clapping didn't you like the poem?" I was so moved I couldn't clap.

Reading Jonas's poems there have been times when I was sure I heard Jonas reading them to me in Lithuanian. Spinoza said: mathematics is everything. I'll put my chip in and say, language is everything.

Pause

There are beasts that are given authority and they take pleasure in being cruel. I remember a matron and a nurse in the boarding school I went to, they were sadists. I was arrested and booked on vagrancy numerous times when I was hitchhiking. City and county jails are overcrowded and my experience was the Sheriff and his Deputies enjoyed humiliating those of us who were locked up. But

I can't imagine what it was like to be a slave or live in a DP camp for years with people who have survived concentration camps.

Pause

Jonas's descriptions of arriving in New York City reminded me that in 1953 I had a cold walk–up apartment on 4th Street between Avenues B and C. When I first moved in I paid $12 a month, it was raised to 14. There were the El, the smoke, no trees, dirty subways, garbage when I got off work. I had the Cedar Bar, and 10th Street's art galleries.

Pause

In 1971 after an absence of 27 years Jonas goes back to Lithuania for a visit. In December of 2017 Martha and I saw a film that he made of that visit. The film begins not in Lithuania but in Williamsburg, Brooklyn where he lived and filmed the back yards, the bricks, people's faces, the laundry flapping in the wind, the traffic and the streams of people crossing the street, all frame the distance between Lithuania and Williamsburg.

Pause

I was a boy in England and for a short time during World War II my mother, my aunt Jenny and my cousin Renee all lived in a very primitive village outside of Northampton. Our cottage had running water but many of the other houses didn't and they obtained their water from a well situated on the village green. I have never seen a farm like Jonas's mother's farm. It was another world, an old one. She cooked on a home-made stove that was outside of the house and it was never explained how she cooked when it rained or when it snowed. The well water was for drinking and bathing, the cow's milk was unpasteurized and there was no indoor plumbing. And yet every one in the movie had clean clothes. The men were shaved and the women's hair looked brushed and clean.

This film like all of his films have continuous quick frame changes and these days the changes in the films are too quick for my eyes. I can't take it. As you know I have Macular Degeneration. During the film I had to keep closing my eyes. But I had no trouble seeing the bucolic beauty of the fields, his brothers and his sister singing and dancing and the affection they shared with their neighbors.

Pause

Back in America Jonas gets up in the morning and fries onions, goes to work, walks the streets, thinks of his friends and the impossibility of love, of peace. He contemplates that people are hopeless, impractical. Jonas has nowhere to go and he doesn't want to leave poetry. Language grips him and Jonas flies! Nature, innovation, desperation, Jonas never inflicts us with formula. Where does the light come from? Butterfly wings and intense labor deliver his memories, Jonas hopes for a miracle.

In his *Daybooks* he ends poem 66 this way:

> I cross
> the ruins
> of poisoned
> earth,
>
> still
> believing

in

miracles.

Pause

Jonas had all the disadvantages of being an immigrant. He had been an immigrant when he was in a factory in Germany doing slave labor. He was an immigrant when he was in the DP camps. He needed to establish new roots and that's not so simple. Root is a word that is overtaxed but to belong, to know your own street corner, it is essential.

December 31, 2017

BASIL KING, born in London, England, before World War II, has been painting for over six decades and writing since 1985. His latest book, *History Now* (Marsh Hawk Press, 2017) is the most recent in his long series *Learning to Draw*. Basil is honored to be the subject of the 2012 film, *Basil King: mirage*, directed by Nicole Peyrafitte and Miles Joris-Peyrafitte. Text in the film is from his book, *Mirage: a poem in 22 sections* (Marsh Hawk Press, 2003), and most images on camera are his art. See more at www.basilking.net.

"I am deeply concerned about the potential for fascism, here and around the world, which I oppose as an artist who brings disparate things together."

Steve Dalachinsky
MEKAS/LENS/ on *Daybooks* and other poems

1.

Jonas Mekas –the role of film / the roll of the poem / line lens EYE > heart > " a joyous tear or one of pain" / SOUL / worker / thinker / lover / the simplicity of that LINE > wisdom / wisecracking / history / his poems like his films are the diaries of his journeys / what he sees / feels / tastes / drinks in / frame by frame / WINE > the youth of ageless YOUTH – frank > natural like the water flowing red that he describes / like the youth he surrounds himself with to keep his blood flowing as his recent poems state > his is the poetry of landscape in life / what is behind the blood that keeps a person alive > neither warm nor cold but there or rather IS … a testament to displacement/placement / not being but belonging / in exile but feeling right at home / never forgetting one's roots / the flowers / the flowing water / the pretty girls / the WINE always back to the red wine of childhood and ageless AGE / a part from and a part of the world / the earth / always a beginner / searcher / nostalgia-memory connected to the whisperer / is always there / creating / "feeling" and forming "history" "over" and over "again" / content and form settling within a field open yet crowded with color / color ever changing to COLORS / always within the HEART of place / hopelessly romantic / relaxed and never frantic / "I'm a lone soul with no place to go …" he claims yet that "no place" is every place / and his is there / all there and always present as the DAYS attest 1 by 1 toward the end time / "… how far yet to my home …" he asks counting upward while counting on the word/image to transport us to that HOME where he/we reside uncomfortably comforted by this longing to miss what will come again … for home is never that far … for home is wherever Jonas is within the poem or without … wherever Jonas resides is HOME … "life's pits / meadows / leftovers." walking / sitting / living in America in its heart in New

York / thinking in Lithuanian … all these lives / these frames / these borders in one SOUL.

2.

Daybooks 1970–72 presents 76 days out of an actual 12 years (1970–1982). or were some of these snapshots written on the same day? are we dealing with a period that encompasses 12 years? why these isolated 76 and are these sketches in chronology? where are all the other months days seconds hours minutes / does it, in fact, matter? are they a narrative or just fragments of time in no particular order the way memory itself tends to be? whatever they are. whatever their chronology they fit together as if indeed they were just that > a poetic diary of 76 days > "I wring my hands …" "I keep pounding on … My own door!" on which days of which of these years did his keen eyes see the branch tips? his keen ears listen to Mozart? "Nothing out of the ordinary from one day to the next," yet just by noticing this, recording this, what Jonas does is both transform and "*elevate the commonplace*," at times giving it a kind of hidden-in-plain sight magic/meaning. but because this is such a wide and scattered chronology my text about this particular work with its uncertainty of dates creates an even more disconcerting and interesting scenario due to the fascinating jumps in this temporal, corporeal, almost ephemeral calendar.

as in > (JUMP CUTS)

what we experience through Vyt Bakaitis's translations is the simple beauty Mekas sees / experiences / breathes and ultimately transforms into poetry / a poetry/poetics as pure / alive / simple and complicated as those things / desires are themselves. like Jonas we should all "stick a book of poems in" our pockets and "take off" never analyzing or trying to figure things out, yet, at the same time, never giving up grappling with or puzzling over those "THINGS" and we/he/one should always maintain being here in the moment whether covering our ears to protect them from the noise of traffic or simply like "words" "slip away in time's stream."

3.

a short summary (the 1990s reprise) and yet again memory repeats itself as Jonas keeps the camera running and as if in dream/montage "nor hands the same, / nor eyes ..." he tumbles "down memory's trail" always remaining intact while in the act of falling / repeating / trailing off / telling his life's story simply eloquently and elegantly / always in flux while grounded. the "Words ... pouring out in scraps." these scraps so important that they appear over and over again / different takes / yet always the same respectful / sadly humorous / stable though wandering EYE. unstable yet constant "Gateways to the past" "all in red / all in red" once again RED. watching the leaves fall / knowing always knowing that we too will "fade." this is such REAL insight into, not just human fragility and strength, but that of LIFE itself "as memory still keeps bleeding." there it is again like that Dali painting *The Persistence of Memory*. the clock always ticking somewhere in the back of one's head. yet time itself is beyond it's own simple face. "time's flimsy whispers." are we dealing here with **time's time** or **man's time**. and as the end draws near just us "in nakedness of sky" surrounded by nature ... those people / those places those stones / the sunlight and moss all there to greet us / "the secrets of little people" of whom Jonas admits "I'm just as small as you are ... a beginner."

coda:

i'll give you this from Mekas's joy and pain ... "My head sags from prowling to salvage scraps of my days." "hint of light/ hair of light / hands of light / song of light." these "scraps" like strips of film / moments in time / precious and precise / the poem of his life where nothing is taken for granted no matter how ordinary it may appear ...

and though he claims early on that "civilization has no poetry." that in fact "the body of poetry has withered" he later states "my poet's cheeks grown pale ..." while at the same time "poetry / scrubs me / body-clean."

so sit. drink your beer. gaze out the window. you're alone. yet you are not. as Jonas offers: "Here's a poem for you."

nyc 11/17-12/17

STEVE DALACHINSKY is a poet/collagist who was born in Brooklyn (1946) after the last big war and has managed to survive lots of little wars. His book *The Final Nite* (Ugly Duckling Presse, 2006) won the PEN Oakland National Book Award. His latest CDs are *The Fallout of Dreams* with Dave Liebman and Richie Beirach (Rogueart, 2014) and *ec(H)o-system* with the French art-rock group, the Snobs (Bam Balam, 2015). He has received both the Kafka and Acker Awards and is a 2014 recipient of a Chevalier D' le Ordre des Artes et Lettres. His poem "Particle Fever" was nominated for a 2015 Pushcart Prize. His books include: *Fools Gold* (Feral Press, 2014), *A Superintendent's Eyes* (revised and expanded 2013/14 - unbearable/autonomedia), *Flying Home*, a collaboration with German visual artist Sig Bang Schmidt (Paris Lit Up Press, 2015), *The Invisible Ray* (Overpass Books, 2015) with artwork by Shalom Neuman, Frozen Heatwave, a collaboration with Yuko Otomo (Luna Bissonte Prods 2017) and *Black Magic* (New Feral Press, 2017). His column "Outtakes" appears regularly in the *Brooklyn Rail.* His most recent release is *With Shelter Gone*, a full length 12" LP on the German label Psych.KG. Most recently, *Where Night and Day Become One: The French Poems*, a selection 1983 – 2017 has been published (Great Weather for Media, 2018).

"i can only hope that in these times (any time) one's work ideals and concepts will prosper & enrich the self & others."

Carter Ratcliff

Jonas Mekas, American: Notes on *Words Apart*

Jonas Mekas published *Words Apart*, a book of his poems in Lithuanian, in 1967. Reappearing this year in a translation by the poet Vyt Bakaitis, the collection feels timely—and that is strange. *Words Apart* is now five decades old; moreover, it testifies to Mekas's thoughts and feelings, his state of being, at an even earlier period: the years just after the Second World War. Having escaped from a Nazi labor camp as the war ended, he settled into the role of philosophy student at the University of Mainz in southwestern Germany. Nonetheless, he felt adrift—psychically, if not literally—until 1949, when he and his brother Adolfas were resettled in Brooklyn by the International Refugee Organization of the United Nations.

Words Apart falls into five sections, all of them divided into subsections of varying length. Mekas's lines are startlingly short. Each contains just a word or two, except for lines that present a hyphenated fragment of a long word. Stanzas, therefore, are extremely thin. The visual effect is of language unfurling into a void, extenuating itself as it goes. There are few metaphors in *Words Apart*, few similes, or poetic devices of any sort. Yet these stripped-down works display none of the narrative or expository impulses that would turn them into prose. They are poems unshaped by poeticisms, utterances addressed to a world where a "man" sits

> deep in
> orchard
> shade
>
> . . . watching
> appletrees

the heat
struck
vibrate,

sky
all
trembling
linden.
(*Words Apart*, I, 3)

A bit later in the book:

There
are
times
I'll
feel
a breeze
fresh

on my
fingers
or
eyes—

and
far
less
often,
drops
of
light,

spray
-ing
sparks,

briefly
throw
light
on the
whole
horizon—
then go
all
dark
again—
(II, 7)

The poet's sharp focus on fugitive sensations illuminates his isolation in self-awareness. His perceptions are all he has, and sometimes these diminish to nearly nothing.

The night
gets
deeper
and
deeper.

I lie
there,
alone,
eyes
open.

Darkness
falls
on black
windows . . .
(IV, 7)

At "noon / -day's / fla- / ming / shore," the poet sits "alone, with no / thoughts / in mind." (IV, 12) As "The sun's / last rays" fall, he is again "alone" at water's edge. (IV, 16) In an unnamed harbor, he stands "alone," looking "at a / city / burning / at noon." (IV, 20)

The word "alone" recurs not as an anguished refrain but as a calm acknowledgement of a fact comparable to the facts delivered by Mekas's observations of rocks and boulders, lighthouses and cafés, a snake only momentarily visible, a bee feeding at leisure on clover. Neither threatened nor engaged, the poet navigates the world with seeming ease, and yet he belongs to it only contingently or perhaps not at all. Tracing a "shoreline, alone," he says that he is "far / from / home, / far / from / home." (IV, 17) For reasons never stated, there is no possibility of return. Mekas is a "lone / soul / with no / place / to go." (IV, 20)

Forsaken by the past, marooned in a present disconnected from any future, the poet has inoculated himself against nostalgia. There is only the moment, inflected by feelings of loneliness, physical sensations, and the visible things—other human beings among them—that give the poems of *Words Apart* their subject matter. These drifting, sometimes flickering phenomena have no backdrop, social, cultural, or historical. Slowly, one realizes how strange this is. Most poems emerge, however circuitously, from a coherent world. Mekas's do not, as the poet is acutely but never bitterly aware.

"In the Woods," the second section of *Words Apart*, begins with this declaration:

I,
too,
now
halfway
through
my life,

entered
a
dark
woods,

lost
track,
saw
no
more
signs . . .
(II, 1)

In this darkness, we see clearly the precision with which Mekas reprises the opening of Dante's *Inferno*. For the earlier poet also speaks of having reached the midpoint of his life and finding himself lost in a dark wood (*selva oscura*), unable to find a clear path (*diritta via*). Soon Dante encounters three beasts—a leopard, a lion, and a she-wolf—each laden with symbolic meanings as sinister as they are obscure. As he continues his journey, symbols proliferate, meanings intertwine, and soon we are enmeshed in a pattern of historical allusion and theological speculation so vast and complex that it takes on the scale and speculative richness of a cosmology.

Mekas's *Words Apart* contains nothing comparable, nor does this book rest, like the *Inferno* and the entire *Divine Comedy*, on a foundation of allusions to earlier poetry. Dante rewrites Plato, Virgil, Augustine, and the entire tradition of medieval Romance. Mekas invokes Dante's "dark wood" to let us know that he rejects the machinery of symbol and literary reference fully and deliberately, in favor of imagery that reflects an immediate, isolated *now*. For this is all that feels real to him, all in the bleak years after the Second World War that has the power to compel his belief. When, toward the end of section IV, Mekas writes

> Day's
> done,
> heart's
> stable.
>
> Here
> lies
> the wine
> -red
> sea
>
> (IV, 19)

it may seem that he softens his rejection of European tradition by acknowledging Homer, who so often describes the sea as "wine-dark." But he is doing the opposite, echoing Homer only to extend to ancient times the range of the cultural inheritance he rejects. From 1949 to the present, Mekas has understood himself as the sort of American who inhabits a fluid, improvised present devoted to the future and its precedent-free possibilities. Mekas realizes these possibilities chiefly in film. He is a major figure in the history of avant-garde cinema in the United States. Yet he has always written—the list of his publications includes diaries, memoirs, and poetry—and his style in both of his mediums has always tended toward unadorned clarity. Hence his filmic and poetic imagery join to make it plausible to see him as a late recruit to Imagism, a movement launched in the 1910s by a small band of American and English poets determined to rescue poetry from the extravagant metaphor and decorative surplus cultivated by late Victorian poets.

The idea of Mekas as an Imagist gains strength from a choice Bakaitis, his translator, made at the outset of *Words Apart*. The Lithuanian title of the book's first section is "Vaizdai," a word that could be rendered in English as "views," "vistas," "appearances," "spectacles," or "images." By choosing the last of these, Bakaitis brings the Imagists to mind and prompts us to ask if Mekas belongs in the company of Ezra Pound, Hilda Doolittle (H. D.), William Carlos Williams, and other members of the group. He does not and, in seeing why not, we see Mekas a bit more clearly.

Passionate reformers, the Imagists insisted that poetry must attain a new clarity, concision, and freedom not only from traditional meter but also from the echoes of metric tradition to be heard in *vers libre*. The goal was specificity. Each conjunction of word and world must record a unique moment of experience.[1] So far, Mekas and the Imagists are in accord. They diverge on the plane of ultimate meaning. Pound wrote in 1918 that "an 'Image' is that which presents an intellectual and emotional complex in an instant of time." If it is truly instantaneous, the 'Image' gives the reader "a sense of freedom from time limits and space limits."[2] It is not obvious, at first glance, how to reconcile these pronouncements with Pound's best-known Imagist poem:

"In a Station of the Metro'"
The apparition of these faces in the crowd;
Petals on a wet, black bough.[3]

For this imagery ushers us into a well-defined place, the Paris Metro, and evokes springtime, the season when trees flower. To feel unconstrained by the poem's "time limits and space limits" we must agree in retrospect with Pound's prediction, made in 1918, about the best poetry of the twentieth century. "Its force," he said, "will lie in its truth."[4]

Pound means neither the truth established by scientific experiment nor that of the ordinary observations that guide us through the world. He appeals to an idea of timelessly transcendent truth—Truth with a capital "T"—that is rooted in Platonism. The Neoplatonist Plotinus, Renaissance, and Baroque theorists, and Romantics of the late eighteenth and early nineteenth centuries all argued that art and literature can be vehicles of—or windows onto—Truth of this exalted kind. And their arguments persist, much revised, in certain strands of modernism. Pound and the other Imagists were, if not strict Neoplatonists, then heirs to this ancient faith. Like Plotinus, they believed that a poem or painting succeeds by revealing an essence: the ultimate, absolute, and immutable Truth of its subject. Mekas signals his awareness of this tradition in "Remnants of a Journey," the third section of *Words Apart*.

During a journey by airplane, he says:

Now
I
know

it's
true:

like
cloud
wisps
I fall,
the night
through.

9.
It's
not
that
I'm
even
so
sure!

As
before,
I just
don't
see
any
brink,

and
I
know
it's
not by

my
own
force
I
fall.

But
I'm
through

looking for
the essence,

or
raising
questions,

and take
all evenly
in
as
a
gift,
with

the same
wonder
at
sun
-sets
as at
humans,

or

the night's

black

-ness.

(III, 8, 9)

With this passage, Mekas renounces the quest for essences. Or, as he says elsewhere, he rejects Europe's "logic and reason" (II, 7)—his metonym for the Platonism that infuses the art of Michelangelo, the poetry of Percy Bysshe Shelley, and the theories of racial essence that provided European fascism with its metaphysical underpinnings. In the aftermath of his and Lithuania's encounters with Nazi Germany, Mekas extricated himself from two and a half millennia of European metaphysics. Thus he joined the company of such American non-metaphysicians as the pragmatist John Dewey, the ironist Andy Warhol, and Merce Cunningham, choreographer of ordinary movement. Separating himself from such New-World seekers of Old-World essences as Ezra Pound and the other Imagists, he became, in a way, more American than they were.

Endnotes

1 Ezra Pound, "Affirmations: As for Imagisme" (1915), reprinted in *Ezra Pound: Early Writings, Poems and Prose*, ed. Ira Nadel, New York: Penguin Books, 2005, pp. 292-96

2 Ezra Pound, "A Retrospect" (1918), reprinted in *Modernism: An Anthology of Sources and* Documents, ed. Vassiliki Kolocontroni, Jane Goldman, Olga Taxidou, Chicago: The University of Chicago Press, 1998, p. 374

3 Ezra Pound, "In a Station of the Metro" (1913), *Personae: The Collected Poems of Ezra Pound*, New York: New Directions, 1926, p. 109

4 Ezra Pound, "A Retrospect," p. 378

CARTER RATCLIFF is a poet and art critic who lists the following among his published books of poetry: *Fever Coast, Give Me Tomorrow*, and *Arrivederci Modernismo*, His books on art include *Andy Warhol, The Fate of a Gesture: Jackson Pollock* *and Postwar American Art*, and *Kit White: Line into Form.* His first novel, *Tequila Mockingbird*, was published in 2015.

"All my writing is driven by the need to generate meaning, whether from scratch, with poetry and fiction, or by responding to the works of others, as in my art criticism."

Kristin Prevallet

"Words Apart": A Mekas Reflection

Part I. Images

Jonas Mekas's eye is a camera and it records images, brief snapshots of people standing in various landscapes, posed in an unconscious moment. As a filmmaker he scans the world looking for these images, and that is what is important. They bring him *into the world.* There is a skipping-rock rhythm to these little poems which record one image after another. Like a snapshot, each image stands alone in a stanza. There is no commentary or urge to describe these images within some sort of narrative. A man stands quietly in the water, mid-stream. Raindrops break into the backyard. A man sits under an apple tree. A bird in the heat of sunlight. A power boat sounds in the distance. Someone sitting on the shore looks down, and then up.

It's just
this image

just this

Part II. Into the Woods

1.

Images may bring Mekas *into the world,* but thinking does the opposite. Now, the poem takes a radical, interior turn. If in Part I images connect the filmmaker to what is happening in the present moment, in Part II thinking does the opposite. It takes the poet into the maze of fragments and their corresponding emotions, all roads leading to the fragmentation of a childhood splintered by war. The images of the present moment may offer a temporary reprieve, but a haunted past is running in the background.

A very skinny poem in eight parts. "Words Apart." Words are broken at their hyphen, which makes reading slow and introspective. Like walking down a path in the forest, but at half-pace. When the heart slows, the rhythm becomes worm-like going deeper, and deeper; down into the darkest part of the woods where thick canopies and dense underbrush make no path visible.

I
too,
now
halfway
through
my life,

entered
a
dark
woods,

lost
track,
saw
no
more
signs,

and
now
have
to
start
all

over

again . . .

Burrowing under the ground, deep and deeper. Where else is there to go but to the source? The mistakes made, the time passed, the people gone. And here he is, just himself, earthen and alone (in the way that trees are solitary, but in good company, within their academies).

2.

Looking, searching, scrambling, wanting, grabbing, coveting. Finding no satisfaction in that endless circling of thoughts that go nowhere and hold nothing for longer than a fleeting second.

Was
all
I drummed
myself
up
for,
for nothing,
nothing at all,
going
deeper,
deeper
in,

going

in
ever
widening
circles,

in
-scribing,
scribing
ever
larger
circles
inside,
trying
and
trying,

again
and
again,
to reach,
reach for
the untold
sense and
purpose
to
my
existence,

Pacing, scribing, trying. Asking, listening, ignoring; believing, touching, piercing. The poem is spliced by its *ings*—they set the pace. He cannot *ing* in silence, which leads him to not believe in it. P*ing*ing around like an atomic cocktail in fusion colliding with every object. He wants to "to corroborate all there is," and yet all that *ing*-ing into things does not appease his anxiety:

inside,
breaking

and
raging,
raging
to escape,

stays
locked up,
un
-told.

3.

It's a funny thing about banging into things when you are not an atomic particle. It hurts, and you risk losing your sense of bodily awareness. Not to mention how angry it makes you when you realize that other people don't seem to be having this problem. And so you return to your mind, to blame it all on thinking. But therein lies the maze, a prison, with no clear way in or out.

All you
people
I've
seen
no
more
into
than
into
things—

seeing
you
merely

as

move

-ment,

po

-etry—

just as

a rain

-drop

will

spill from

a brim

-ming

cloud,

not

of

its own

force,

or

heat,

yet

in

-sep

-erable

from

both.

4.

A Dream I call here, not vain Dreams, or idle imaginations: for those are vain, and have no Divination in them, but arise from the remains of watchings, and disturbance of the body.

> For as the mind is taken up about, and wearied with cares, it suggests itself to him that is asleep.[1]

Dreams of the past, of all the people whose paths we crossed—all the backyard gatherings with friends sitting around in a circle, eating, watching the children play, playing croquet, running, jumping on the beach, at Montauk those gentle waves, those bodies, in the evening we sat around the fireplace talking about the Occult, De Kooning, and the next great party; we had picnics on the Williamsburg bridge above the industrial East River, we leaned into each other, shared strawberries, and now all of that is captured, one shaking frame after another, fragments assembled like memories themselves, hard to grab hold of a story, just the facts—that there we were. These are the dreams that are the remains of watching; the dreams that now disturb the body.

and
I
don't know
where
we are
now,

what
distance
or
nearness
we
share,

if it's
language

of matter
or
of spirit
we
speak—

the con
-spiracy
of things
I'm
trying
to
break
free of—

my
heart's
own
impul
-ses
drive
me
to

disrupt
my
rhythms
and
constantly

confine me
to

the heart
of space,

without
reprieve.

5.

What is the poetry of exile? Writing on Czesław Miłosz in *The Nation*, Terrence Des Pres writes: "In exile from a world which no longer exists, [his] poetry [confronts] the central issues of our time: the impact of history upon moral being, the search for ways to survive spiritual ruin in a ruined world."[2]

Mekas too is in exile, as Europe "scattered my childhood," leaving him to carry the ruins in his body and in his memory. The impact of this scattering is the uncertainty of surrendering to time's passing but never feeling fully healed by it.

To a child, an hour goes on forever. This is because they are not yet living in the past. As people grow older, they might say, "time goes by so fast," but this is because they are living in their mind, reflecting on a time that has already gone by. If they were to look to the future, to time that is still evolving, it would slow down again.

This is the thought that preoccupied me as I sat for three hours watching Mekas's film *He Stands in the Desert Counting the Seconds of his Life* (1986). A shaking of every image is quickly spliced; it is impossible to grab hold of a moment for very long; nothing is fixed; time is always moving. Three hours of jiggly home movies because the ground is permanently shifting—in this film he captures not fragments of human tracings onto landscapes, as people come together for gatherings and then move apart into solitude. He captures time itself.

The pleasure in looking at this film comes from soft focus—if in most movies you are straining to make meaning out of a narrative, with Mekas, like meditation, you are simply observing your experience of watching the film, not committing to any one image over another.

This poem is observing itself watching the movies-in-the-mind of the past. Doing this does not make the observer happy. It makes him the opposite.

6.

There is a startling optimism to the film, *He Stands in a Desert Counting the Seconds of his Life* (1986). It moves so quickly between scenes, most of them of parties, or backyard gatherings, sunset cruises on the Hudson, or picnics on the Williamsburg bridge. There are a few scenes of the camera, alone, filming a scene outside a window; some happening like sudden police activity. But most of the film is all about people—the deep conversations, the shared food, the building of history, and time well spent.

The poem turns Mekas towards what is introspective; turns his soul to ruminate on ghosts of the past. The poem descends into the labyrinth of deep thinking; turns against itself—too much is lost. Too much time has passed with no solid footing into the present:

> Looking
> at
> my
> hand,
>
> the

veins
twisting—

un
-able
to
solve
life's
rid
-dling

si
-lence,
I sink
deeper
in.

7.

Silence has become Mekas's enemy. Europe, like the brutal Minotaur, lives there in the shadows, waiting to pull him deep into his core trauma. He knows that casting breadcrumbs into the dark is the only way out, and so he begins focusing on the tiniest parts of words, where they break syllabically:

pre
-positions,
pro-
positions,
words,
things—

start

out
word
by word,
thought
by thought,
act
by act,

and try
to build
myself
up

by leaving
everything
open,

with no
assumed
direc
-tion—

This slow process of building from a foundation that has been shattered, a childhood that knew no security—all he can do is surrender to the thing that he is the most afraid of: uncertainty, impermanence, and the nothing that is a breeze passing by his cheek; the stroke of sunlight in a dark room. Those momentary cracks in dark thinking.

8.

If only he could follow those cracks into the place where they break open and let in all the light. But not in this poem. It ends where it began, trapped in the no-way-out circle of hopelessness.

But there are always the images; always the present. One has faith that Mekas does not stop here, but keeps it turning, always returning to what matters most.

Endnotes

1 From *Three Books of Occult Philosophy, or of Magick*; by Heinrich Cornelius Agrippa. (Digital edition by Joseph H. Peterson, http://www.esotericarchives.com/agrippa/agrippa1.htm, 2000).

2 From *The Nation*, December 30, 1978, p.741.

KRISTIN PREVALLET is a mindbody coach, poet, and educator. She is the author of five books of cross-genre poetry, including the fragmented memoir *I, Afterlife: Essay in Mourning Time* (Essay Press) and *Everywhere Here and in Brooklyn* (Belladonna). She has received residencies and awards from NYFA, Spalding University, Poet's House, the Centre Internationale de Poesie, and the Ocean State Writer's Conference, to name a few. She lives in Westchester where she teaches for Bard College's Prison Initiative, leads workshops on trance writing and Mindbody healing, and works with private clients.

"Preoccupied as I am with maintaining my focus, awareness, and service to the splintering of people's lives during this time of intense upheaval, I'll remain active and of help to as many people as possible, without being submerged."

George Quasha
The Mekas Effect

Jonas Mekas. Saying the name brings home a range of agitating mind sensations, mainly an accumulation of often challenging film experience from the last half-century. Practically a rubric for the whole phenomenon of radically new cinema, it's an *experienced* name, coming to us with compressed suggestion—that is, a name with its own poetics. If saying it now resonates for me in new ways without entirely losing the old ways, it's on account of having read his poetry. Thanks to newly available versions by poet Vyt Bakaitis,[1] which happily give the feel of primary texts in English, we quickly forget we're reading translations. At the same time they remind me that poetry, like film, is inherently translational as well as transformative and that at a certain level of intensity all language is foreign. Viewing Mekas's films after reading his poetry I see far better what before I saw at best minimally, even though the films are part of my experience of so many decades, going back to when I was a graduate student living on the Lower East Side. All along, the films have been rather provocative to one's own aesthetic tendencies and complexly instructive, and now this is true in dimensionally new ways. In part, no doubt, this is because I *see* differently, but it's also because I recognize the poetry and the films as co-configurative—a single interactive art reality. Mekas's famous "poetic cinema" is far more than a wishful description; it's a declaration of poetics.

This notion of poetry-film as co-configuration is not in the abstract a particularly new observation about Mekas—he himself and indeed others have observed as much in a variety of ways. Some translations of the poetry have been available for years and have not gone unappreciated, yet clearly for many of us they haven't made it to the forefront of Mekas awareness. That may change if, experiencing the work from 2018 on, with so much of the poetry now at hand, it makes a difference worth further distinction. And that difference, especially the emergent impact on how we see the films, itself comes as embodiment of a certain Mekas effect: the persistent and driving force of the work in both film and poetry, which keeps it going in the maker's '90s, and, for us, keeps it a renewable resource—a matrix of further engagement. Unanticipated dimensions flicker into view.

These are notes in medias res, as I'm reporting on the work provisionally, from a rather new perspective for me, still in process of a full re-experiencing. But then Mekas's work itself is always and only in the middle of its dark woods, using available light to shed further light. "Words Apart" plays on Dante's opening:

> I
> too,
> now
> halfway
> through
> my life,
>
> entered
> a
> dark
> woods . . .[2]

At core the work is driven in large part by an impulse toward embrace and the darkening/enlightening interruptions along the way. Some call this tendency Romantic, a term Mekas himself considers as early as the World War II diaries of *I Had Nowhere to Go,*[3] and there are of course historical aspects of Romanticism that embody a related impulse, variously construed. We read:

> *March 28th 1948 . . .*
> Ah, you, realists! I am not ashamed of my romanticism.
>
> Ah, you abstractionists: I will confess to you my passion for objects, earth, nature.
>
> Should I pretend I am a stone when emotions, memories surge and overflow me, and I am dreaming of home, and melting snows?

Even recently he affirms: "All my work, with the exception of the *Destruction Quartet*, is a celebration of life around me, a celebration of life in its different joyful manifestations."[4] Yet it matters greatly what the embrace includes, what it produces, and how it evolves through actual practice. Central to that practice is quite a lot of visual content hardly considered by many to be beautiful or even palatable, ranging from ordinary to abrasive and including the harsher, visually challenging images of *Destruction Quartet. Mekas confirms his belief* that "destruction has its own positive, unfathomable reason of being. Destruction of the Berlin Wall was certainly a positive event. *Destruction Quartet* is a meditation on four different aspects of destruction."[5] The installation of four unsynchronized simultaneous films with footage of very different kinds of violence,6 allowing a range of implications, goes far outside, say, the "Poetry Is a Destructive Force" aesthetic frame of Wallace Stevens, yet retains a sense of art as the transformative alternative to actual violence. Art may still function at the meta level that can handle a troubled world and offer a means of embracing life. There is a complexity in the actual art happening that stands well beyond a classification like Romantic or otherwise. The closer one gets to Mekas overall, the less one feels able to frame the work.

It's interesting to notice that, in our conceptually refocused sense of art values, we use the name *Romantic* for a basic exuberance about living and a commitment to engage negative experience with energy and direct attention. This is not to deny the usefulness of such observations at specific angles, such as that of P. Adams Sitney addressing a diary film like *Reminiscences of a Journey to Lithuania* (1972) as "Romantic autobiography," where "Mekas constantly weaves together celebrations of the present moment, immediately and unironically present on the screen, with elegiac and ironic allusions to a presence that is forever absent to the camera lens: the vision of nature and his childhood."[7] There are many such instances in the poetry, in particular a work of the same period as the film *Reminiscences*; there's *Daybooks: 1970 – 72,*[8] for instance, where the weave of perceptions, times, sentiments, vocal tonalities creates a complex time-surface, drawing close while cutting loose:

56
Full light of
paradise
still shines
behind your
silk
lashes.

Your face
mild as
milk.
All too soon
incredulity
strikes,
light
-ning
like,

shattering
the tree
of paradise.

Lashing
gusts
will be
flailing
redemption.

The short lines give a frame-by-frame tension to shifting apperception; the ecstatic and high-minded mesh with the concrete and evanescent; and each poem in the sequence further suggests a variant orientation and time ambiguity:

59.
sun,
O sun

with my hands
to my face
I kneel
before a dried-up
childhood

riverbed.

The stanza break between frame-lines—"childhood" and "riverbed"—sequences our (ap)perception so that the interior sense of a lost youthful world (childhood frame) has immediate impact as the actual concrete thing experienced (riverbed frame). In the films the speed of frame sequence fragments the affective object so that the feel of a thing shown is displaced across time, interruptively; in the poem, the short framing lines mete out the affective qualities slowly. Intensity by speed as against slowing intensity—two kinds of articulation by sharp blockings in the flow.

This sense of performative complexity in the art-embrace no doubt has roots in the survival function of poetry for Mekas—life interruptions and blockages in the harsh war experience of exile from Lithuania and nearly five years internment, first as eight months in a German labor camp followed by some four years in the DP (displaced persons) camps, recounted in *I Had Nowhere to Go*: "You live because you want to write a poem. We write poems because if we didn't, we couldn't live. To be or not to be. To write or not to write."[9] Variations on this theme have played throughout his life, and when it comes to film, as in the three-hour *Walden* (*Diaries, Notes, and Sketches*) (1969), he narrates: "I live, therefore I make films. I make films, therefore I live. Life. Movement. I make home movies, therefore I live. I live, therefore I make home movies." The modulation of *voice* of the diaries, of the poems, and of the films share a "poetic" register—actual tones of *physical* voice as well—and comprise a binding force at the center of both work and personal life. That continuously manifesting voice conveys a sense of unflinching faith in poietic process and allows him to speak of "poetic film" with a meaning of the transformative and life-awakening complexity of poiesis itself. It's a big part of what strikes me as the Mekas effect in diary, poem, or film.

Clearly the artist we know as one of the most challenging and influential filmmakers himself identifies first of all as poet, and the obsession with reading, writing, editing, and poetry holds to the center of concern right along; and that self-identification stays pretty much on a par with basic survival in the war/"displaced person" diaries.

Practically the first words of the diary, July 19, 1944, eight days after setting out to escape the perils of occupied Lithuania: "I am neither a soldier nor a partisan. I am neither physically nor mentally fit for such life. I am a poet."[10] Arriving in America was scarcely a deliverance from hardship—a sense of alienation, job problems, numbing factory work, wondering why he should keep writing in a language no one will read—yet the diaries continue. Within weeks Jonas and his brother Adolfas are borrowing cameras, filming, seeking out experimental film clubs, and two months after arriving, they borrow money and buy their first Bolex 16. Diary poetics finds a new home in film. Now writing and filming run side-by-side, an intrinsic double-screen with unpredictable synchrony.

Of course, the notion of poet-filmmaker is not unknown in the film world Mekas has celebrated and advanced, notably in his influential *Village Voice* "Movie Journal,"[11] and in what became Anthology Film Archives. Among his contemporaries one thinks not only of "experimental" filmmakers who actually have written poetry as part of their core work, such as James Broughton, but of more widely celebrated European filmmakers like Cocteau and Pasolini. A filmmaker at the level of Stan Brakhage, who was a powerful writer and in fact deeply immersed in poetry from the start, is a poet in Mekas's actual sense of the word: his film language had the intensity and structural integrity as an "art of vision."[12] And this is the sense of *poetic* that keeps the word alive in any modality of creative work with words, film, or other extensions of *language* in its real art meaning.

If we wonder how a poet can also be an artist at a high level of realization, it's that we are mainly seeing poetry and visual art in terms of the differences between the mediums; and this of course must be foregrounded in understanding an art form's operative principles and impact. Yet where multiple arts follow the same intrinsic principle, there is intermedial connection beyond the differences that show up at the level of medium, the physical manifestation of the art. And also there is art as lived and worked through in a fuller sense—the *whole* art. I regard an art as whole *within* what issues from its impulse to extend a core principle, but not necessarily in all that gathers at the periphery. Mekas has consistently grounded work in his own immediate focus, a principled journeying without plan or scenario, to the extent that, in his conversation with Brakhage in 2000, he playfully calls himself a *filmer* rather than a filmmaker: "I sometimes joke, I say I am not really a filmmaker; I am only a filmer. I film real life. I never know what will come next. The shape of my films emerges from the accumulation of the material itself. I go through my life with my Bolex camera."[13] If sticking to principle requires a stalwart contrarian nature, Mekas may be at the head of the pack:

> They all say yes.
> But I'll say no,
> from basic principle,
> like salt.
>
> (*Daybooks* #10)

He also goes through life speaking. Words and film are orientational and situational, and they are themselves localities of responsive equivalence. They stand in, with, for, and up against what presents itself in the immediacy of experience. And it's all in motion. He identifies both film and poetry as movement, and both show up through a frame-rate. It's as though the experience of the single-frame button on the Bolex 16, which had such an influence on how filmmakers like Mekas used the camera, carried over into *verse,* a tightly framed "turning over" of lines:

> At times,

it seems
I'm
so
close,
close
to
things,

I tremble
on touching
my foot to
the earth.

All you
people
I've
seen
no
more
into
than
into
things—

seeing
you
merely
as
move
-ment,
po
-etry—. . . .

There is thinking that finds its way only in alignment with movement, and Jonas Mekas has explored this core principle, the primacy of movement in poetry and film, as something approaching a life mission. Camera in hand is bodymind knowing by getting in step with what is happening, the current of things.[14] "Poetic cinema" becomes what, historically, its first instrument suggested in the name *cinematograph*—literally, *writing motion*, from Greek *kinema*, "motion." Notably the *O.E.D.*, which prefers the spelling *kinematograph*, calls it a "contrivance (invented by Messrs. Lumière of Paris) by which a series of instantaneous photographs taken in rapid succession can be projected on a screen with similar rapidity, so as to give a life-like reproduction of the original moving scene." Mekas both as filmmaker and poet seems to see the world in frames, instant images or verbal units in motion, created particle-objects embodying *takes*—takes *on* and *from* the moving reality of living—rapid-fire equivalences in projection. Projector and screen, book and page, the instruments of viewing, set an intensely refocused world in motion before eye-mind. One might say projective verse mirrors projective film.[15]

Whatever comes into play has its own rhythmic interlace with the immediate as viewed against the absent. Memory, primarily as nostalgia, comes as internal pressure on the moment, shaping the sense of presence against what is missing. The issue of redemption as reclaiming what is lost in a transforming present includes an acknowledgment of irredeemability—"flailing redemption." "My head sags," he says in *Daybooks* #8, "from prowling / to salvage / scraps / of my days." The past as the experience of loss is the underside of the present as loss of self-purpose, an ontological crisis that runs beneath everything; it's a pervasive disruption in "Words Apart":

> the con
> -spiracy

of things
I'm
trying
to
break
free of—

my
heart's
own
impul
-ses
drive
me
to

disrupt
my
rhythms
and
constantly

confine me
to
the heart
of space,

without
reprieve.
("In the Woods" #4)

Memory, indeed nostalgia, is never as simple as the word suggests, and the actual redemptive force in the Mekas poetics may be the recovery of lost or damaged language—a parallel to Mallarmé's renovated words of the tribe—which, without poiesis, becomes a "mind forg'd manacle" (Blake) and an emotional slide, the way we lean into abstract understanding. The power of his poem or film is as much in what it strips away as in what it presents, isolating us in any impatient need of resolution.

The thin, short-lined poems that stream down the page have a sort of flicker-effect over time, somewhat as the filmic discontinuous splicing's temporal overlays create a "continuous present" (Gertrude Stein) or a sense that "all times are contemporaneous in the mind" (Ezra Pound). There's a linearity that throws us back on the verticality of charged experience. Mekas said recently:

> I work completely linearly. I film, I videotape, day after day, and I string all those pieces together, and when they are seen, they are seen in linear time, second after second after second. But my living — much of the time I do not live in a linear way. I live ecstatically! Vertically![16]

He sometimes speaks of his creative process in meditative terms, and my sense of his work's interruptive temporality is that it calls on the reader/viewer to discover that species of ecstasy, even amidst destruction. And that's another word, like memory, that can have radically new meaning as a poietically focused singularity, a zone of less and less certainty, potentially a zero point or a still point in motion, that opens a space of actual renewal.

Poetry is a state of being, of attitude. It's an exalted, ecstatic state of living, of seeing, of experiencing: [an] intense, intensified way of seeing, perceiving reality, both in art and living. There is poetry in literature, in cinema, in dance, in all of the arts. In literature, haiku form is the most condensed form. Many different emotions and experiences of real life are locked in those few syllables.

It may be an incursion from outside any reliable understanding of memory, destruction, the past, its loss, and indeed aesthetic precedent:

> All of my past is in me. And whatever I do is determined and tinted by it. But there are also things in me that were inherited or given to me by angels, which are completely out of my control. Whatever I do is a product of both earth and heaven. I try to be completely with earth, to live and work instant by instant, in the present moment—that's where my diaristic preoccupations come from. The heaven part I cannot control.[17]

This aspect of Jonas Mekas is no doubt the least obvious. His art of vision is also a very particular art of reading, one that requires the poetry for full instruction in how to do it. *Poetic* also means that a singular art of reading/listening/seeing is implicit in the work. One finds it everywhere in Mekas's work—poetry or film—by way of an open engagement and a reflective state of attention, embracing it all, including his pervasive reentry into the dark night of the soul. The Mekas art is not about resolution or transcendence but a certain energy, performativity, and transmission of possibility. The poetics inheres in a principle of consciously staying with the oscillation between extremes—the past and its loss, the paradisiacal and its disappearance, peaks and vales—as the opportunity for both reflection and further being. In this sense his art is "mimetic" not in how it represents something either exterior or interior but in the state of receptivity itself, what it imparts to one who gets with its open process. To fully reach that alignment we need the poems.

Endnotes

1 Jonas Mekas, *Words Apart and Others*: Poems 1967/1998, bi-lingual edition with translations from the Lithuanian by Vyt Bakaitis, Brooklyn NY: Rail Editions, 2018.

2 Ibid.

3 (New York: Black Thistle Press, 1991), 161

4 Interview with Monica Uszerowicz, "Jonas Mekas on the Poetry of Filmmaking and Living," *Hyperallergic*, March 24, 2016, https://hyperallergic.com/285397/jonas-mekas-on-the-poetry-of-filmmaking-and-living/. (Hereafter "Uszerowicz," n.p.)

5 Uszerowicz.

6 "The videos consist of footage from the demolition of the Berlin Wall in 1990, Danius Kesminas's 1991 fire sculpture, *(New York) Consequence*, a 1997 Nam June Paik performance in which Paik wrecks a piano, and the 2001 destruction of the World Trade Center from the roof of Mekas's SoHo apartment building." See http://jonasmekas.com/exhibitions/?show=-2009fuentes and the press release there.

7 *Visionary Film: The American Avant-Garde, 1943-2000* (Oxford: Oxford University Press, 2002), 339

8 (Brooklyn NY: Portable Press at Yo-Yo Labs, 2003)

9 *I Had Nowhere to Go,* 168.

10 Ibid, 21.

11 Collected in *Movie Journal: The Rise of New American Cinema, 1959-1971*, ed. with intro. Gregory Smulewicz-Zucker, foreword Peter Bogdanovich (New York: Film and Culture Series, Columbia University Press, 2016).

12 The title of a major film by Brakhage, *The Art of Vision* (1965), a further editing of the material in *Dog Star Man* (1961 – 64). Charles Stein reminds me that the poet Robert Kelly suggested the "art of vision" title to Brakhage; the latter recounts this in an unpublished interview with P. Adams Sitney quoted in *Visionary Film,* 204.

13 "A Conversation between Jonas Mekas and Stan Brakhage," which took place at Anthology Film Archives, in New York, on November 3, 2000: http://www.logosjournal.com/brakhage_mekas.htm.

14 This emphasis applies to Brakhage and others as well. The film-poetry view of the primacy of motion/movement has important parallels in dance/body-focused phenomenology, the major proponent of which is Maxine Sheets-Johnstone; see esp. *The Primacy of Movement* (Amsterdam/Philadelphia: John Benjamins Company, 2011).

15 I don't know the extent of Mekas's interest in Charles Olson, whom he mentions in the Brakhage conversation (previous note), and "Projective Verse," but the emphasis on motion and the muscular freedom of "projective" speaking in the verse seem quite related. The rhythmic weave retains the feel of being *uttered* and full-bodied, in either medium.

16 This and following prose quotes are from Uszerowicz.

17 In the same interview Mekas gets even more explicit in the encouraging turn of mind: ". . . I have read my Jakob Boehme, and I have read all the prophets, and I have heard whispers of flowers and winds and songs of birds . . .—so I know that there is something much stronger, much more unfathomable, than us, the humans. So do not despair!"

GEORGE QUASHA, artist/poet/musician, explores an extra-medium principle in language, paint-drawing, sculpture, video, sound, and performance. Awarded a Guggenheim Fellowship (2006), his video art includes *art is: Speaking Portraits,* recording over a thousand artists/poets/composers in eleven countries (saying what art/music/poetry is). Along with the theory of *principle art*, work is presented in the books *Axial Stones: An Art of Precarious Balance* (foreword by Carter Ratcliff) and *art is (Speaking Portraits)* (2016). His twenty books also include, in poetry, *Glossodelia Attract (preverbs)* (2015), *The Daimon of the Moment (preverbs)* (2015), *Things Done for Themselves (preverbs) (2015)*, *Verbal Paradise (preverbs)* (2011), *Ainu Dreams* (1999, with Chie [Hasegawa] Hammons), and *Somapoetics* (1973); and, about art, *An Art of Limina: Gary Hill's Works and Writings* (2009, with Charles Stein; foreword by Lynne Cooke). Recipient of an NEA Fellowship (poetry), he is co-publisher with Susan Quasha at Station Hill of Barrytown. Work at: quasha.com and vimeo.com.

"As poiesis for me is at the center of anything realized, I track a principle I call *axial* in whatever medium presents itself, including the body, to flesh out singularity in a psychonautic sort of way."

Bob Holman

For Jonas Mekas: All Covered in Blue Distances

We
all
know
Jonas's
poems
stretch
through
time

the way
his films
do.

One
word
follows
another

the way
one
image
or one
eye
or
two

eyes
eye

the dancer.

In
Lithuanian
are too
many
syllables
but it
makes
a
nice
display

especially
the case
endings.

2.
No
kidding
around
the way
his play
fullness
absconds
with
the
poem
right
in
the mid
dle of

the film.

3.
No
matter
who
holds
the camera
it is
always
pointed
at you

Dear
Reader
dear
Jonas

4.
Running
into
Jonas
running
through
Tompkins
Square Park

is
to be
the
poem
always

writing
itself
unspooling
black
16mm
film
a path
of seeing
seen.

5.
Regardless
regarding
the image
immaterial
a blue
cloud
entering
the
frame
just
where
he
left
it it
picks
back
up

loops
a whirl
movement

is it
self
the image

the cloud
covers
is
the cloud.

6\.
No
matter
where
the poem
lands
the
camera
is
there
to
catch
it.

7\.
For
his
final
poem

the film
will be
a song

not to
be
sung

Look
Jonas
look
at
the
song
and
see
it
singing
unfolding
song.

BOB HOLMAN is the founder of the Bowery Poetry Club and the author of 17 poetry collections (print/audio/video), most recently *The Cutouts (Matisse)* (PeKaBoo Press) and *Sing This One Back to Me* (Coffee House Press). Bob Holman has taught at Princeton, Columbia, NYU, Bard, and The New School. As the original Slam Master and a director at the Nuyorican Poets Cafe, creator of the world's first spoken word poetry record label, Mouth Almighty/Mercury, and the Artistic Director of the Bowery Poetry Club, Holman has played a central role in the spoken word, slam and digital poetry movements of the last several decades, work that continues with the founding of Bowery Poetry Studios, where he hosts the poetry podcast "Mouth Almighty." A co-founder and co-director of the Endangered Language Alliance, Holman's study of hip-hop and West African oral traditions led to his current work with endangered languages. He is the producer/director/host of various films, including *The United States of Poetry* and *On the Road with Bob Holman*. His film, *Language Matters with Bob Holman*, winner of the Berkeley

Film Festival's Documentary of the Year award, was produced by David Grubin and aired nationally on PBS. Holman traveled for the film and led workshops at language revitalization centers across Alaska and Hawaii, sponsored by the Ford Foundation. His short film, *Khonsay: Poem of Many Tongues*, has lines of poetry in 50 languages, and premiered at the Margaret Mead Film Festival. In 2018, Holman was awarded the Chambra d'Oc Premio Ostana Award for his work in language revitalization. His roots are in Harlan KY, and he currently lives on the Bowery in New York City.

"When hiphop met slam, and spoken word, poetry's origin, became poetry again, I thought my work was done, but now as I see the oral languages of the world rapidly vanishing, I see languages themselves as focus of concern—no language, no poetry, no life."

Benjamin Sloan

Without Any Constraints: Several Shorter Untitled Poems by Jonas Mekas in the Company of Aharon Appelfeld

Blunt is a good word to describe the shorter untitled poems by Jonas Mekas (translated by Vyt Bakaitis), buffeting us as they do between our blood-stained history and a summer day's "white-edged cloud puffs." As I re-read these pieces I was reminded of a near contemporary of Mekas, Aharon Appelfeld—and at first I wasn't quite sure why, but then I realized these two writers have much in common. Mekas was born in 1922 in Lithuania and Appelfeld was born in 1932 in Romania; they both served time in Nazi camps; they each ended up far from where they started, Appelfeld in Israel and Mekas in the United States; and both are accomplished authors, Appelfeld a novelist and Mekas a poet. Given their shared experience, I am going to explore several short poems by Jonas Mekas and draw into the discussion in each case related material from Aharon Appelfeld's memoir, *The Story of a Life*,[1] as well as a novel, *Blooms of Darkness*.[2]

1

You go on to feel
history o
-ver
again.

You go on to feel
blood
under
your feet.

Jagged edges distinguish these shorter poems, the broken-offness of experience suggested in the way this one "o / -ver" breaks. There is something unsettling or jarring in this. However, the poem's opening words "You go on to feel" are reassuring not only because they are the repeated head-piece for each stanza, but also given their direct meaning—that we're *not done*, thank goodness, yet! So far so good, but what we feel is "history" and its "blood / under your feet." The use of the second person is interesting, making Mekas's experience our own, *our* shared world, *our* feet—our tragic history. Around every corner there seems to be this pleasure/pain doubleness, suggested in this case by the "blood / under your feet" and the idea that, sure, this is the blood of history under our feet we are feeling (some of it no doubt our own dripping down!) but hell, at least we are still upright and on our feet. History's blood spilling into the present stands out in Appelfeld's work as well, as we see in this paragraph:

> I do not pretend to be a messenger, a chronicler of the war, or a know-it-all. I feel attached to the places I have lived in, and I write about them. I don't feel that I write about the past. Pure and unadulterated, the past is no more than good raw material for literature. Literature is an enduring present—not in a journalistic sense, but as an attempt to bring time into an ongoing present.[3]

2

I write
with
-out any constraints.

Content and form will
settle
the field.

Memory
still
keeps bleeding.

As these short unadorned direct sentences march down the page we follow along—while at the same time swinging horizontally between one-syllable-lines contrasted with outrushing word strings. Meanwhile, turning experience into meaning, at the core of it all is a three-part collaboration: memory, content/form, and the author sitting in the driver's seat. If memory will just keep "bleeding" (as of course it will), and at the same time "I" can keep writing "with / -out any constraints," then it is up to the "content and form" to "settle / the field." It all works—painful though some of it is—in the way "you go on to feel." Okay. Fine. The process is both simple and complex, rough and smooth, the resulting texture pure Mekas. Reading this poem, I was reminded of this from Appelfeld:

> I've carried with me my mistrust of words from those [WWII] years. A fluent stream of words awakens suspicion within me. I prefer stuttering, for in stuttering I hear the friction and the disquiet, the effort to purge impurities from the words, the desire to offer something from inside you. Smooth, fluent sentences leave me with a feeling of uncleanness, of order that hides emptiness.[4]

3

Ah, we were sitting
in the summer
flowers
and listening
to time's
flimsy whispers.

Along frail
white-edged cloud puffs
a clear
ringing sound

of the
rowdy young larks.

Direct experience and the right words with which to seize it—in this case, "flimsy," "frail / white-edged . . . puffs," "clear / ringing," and "rowdy"—pull the reader by the hair, as it were (though gently), into the poem's moment. And we can't help but notice the tip of the hat to William Carlos Williams's red wheelbarrow "beside the white / chickens." Time and history are always with us, but here sharing an experience with another person turns them (time and history) into "flimsy whispers," thank goodness. Pure immediate sensual shared pleasures, the sounds and sights of a summer day, rest in the one syllable sitting like a cherry atop it all: "Ah." The someone we are with, someone we care about, makes all the difference, finally. So here again, Appelfeld:

> It took me years to return to the embrace of my loyal, good friends, who knew that a person is no more than a bundle of weaknesses and fears, and that there's no need to add to them. If they know the right word to say, they hold it out to you like a slice of bread during a war. And if they don't they sit beside you in silence.[5]

4

I go,
looking at leaves that keep
falling.

Thinking. That we

will fade.
Become
that
coming
feast.

The repeat of "-ing" sets up one rhythm—looking, falling, thinking, coming—as we both take in and are *ourselves*, eventually, the "feast." Words, each one its detachable self, are the leaves "falling" down the page into the final "feast" enjoyed by us the readers doing the "looking." This poem seems to be Mekas's take on the haiku, a nod in this case to Basho, his nature-centered attention paid to the here-and-now, the hopefulness and pleasure therein. Part of the pleasure here resides in the contrast of the quick snap of the shorter lines with the outrushing longer passages ("looking at leaves that keep"). And layering over it all is the rhythmic play of punctuation—for example, the period after "Thinking." Here the oddly placed end-stop pushes back against the mind's forward-rushing meaning-eating desire to move on—especially given the way "That," by its very nature, is a pointing finger, a word whose purpose is to connect what comes before with what follows.

The joy of watching autumn leaves fall ("looking") contrasts with the realization (the "Thinking" part) that ("That") we too will fall, "fade," and die.

5

in your eyes there are
blossoms

of summer
roses,

with time
and
anguish

In these shorter untitled poems by Mekas, one returns repeatedly to an immanent paradox built directly into the texture, the core, of the writing. To bring out this point I will turn to Aharon Appelfeld and how in Chapter Eight of *The Story of A Life*, and in more detail in his novel *Blooms of Darkness*, we read the story of a young boy (one fictional, one autobiographical, both Appelfeld) who survives the roving Nazi troops thanks to his having moved in with a prostitute. Having escaped—by means of no less than a death march— from a work camp where he and his father had been taken, Appelfeld lived in the forest for a time before knocking on a particular door chosen because there were no mean dogs guarding it. The woman was surprised at first but allowed him in and put him to work running errands and doing chores, and in return, he was allowed to live in her walk-in closet. Because he was eight years old and naïve, having previously lived a sheltered middle-class existence, he was confused when he heard Maria (as he refers to her in *The Story of A Life*) meeting with "clients," their whispers interspersed with long silences leading sometimes to screams, slaps, the breaking of glass. She could be generous and even sweet to Aharon, this against the background of troops sweeping the neighborhood searching for Jews they would execute in the town square. A good part of her income came from servicing these same troops. Consuming large quantities of vodka in order to endure these difficult times, Maria could also be cruel:

> The vodka, the men, and the ranting would tire her out, and then she would sleep in, sometimes till late in the afternoon. Sleep did her good. She would get out of bed light and youthful and would start to hum. I would serve her a mug of coffee, and she would call me her "foolish

lambkin," for my hair was curly then. Sometimes she would give my bottom an affectionate pinch. I loved her good moods, and I was afraid of her depressions. [. . .]

Maria's happy spells would fill the hut with a wonderful light, but her depressions were more powerful than her happiness. They were deep and lingering, and they could instantly darken the hut. In one of her black moods she shouted at me, "Bastard, son of bastards! Liar, son of liars! I'll cut your throat with a kitchen knife!"[6]

In Mekas's poem reproduced at the head of this section (#5), the "blossoms / of summer roses" are directly identified "with time / and / anguish"—all of these (the roses, time, anguish) existing simultaneously in "your eyes." There are no capital letters here, as there are in the other short poems, making it feel more than ever like a broken-off fragment, sharp to the touch. We cannot help but wonder who the "eyes" belong to—perhaps someone standing just off stage? On rereading it seems more likely these are our, the reader's, "eyes." If it is us, and we include the entire human race, then it is in "us" that these contrasting ideas, "blossoms" and "anguish," exist together, one identified with the other— much light is mixed with dark in the title of Aharon Appelfeld's novel, *Blooms of Darkness.*

6

Red is a color that surfaces repeatedly in these poems—in roses, in blood, and in the sunset in the following poem:

Along the bay,
high
on the
cragline,

the last
of the sun's
rays come
dropping down,

all in red,
all in red.

Sunset is another end point, like the leaves drifting to the forest floor in the poem ending with the word "feast." For Mekas the red of a sunset is also the blood you "feel . . . under / your feet," the anguish mixed inextricably with the "summer roses."

Mekas strips experience down to a raw center, memory bleeding history. At the same time as we move through these poems we enjoy the lush life, thankful for those sitting beside us amongst the summer roses. It is confusing, the bitter co-existing with the sweet, in others, in us, in everything, but it cannot be any other way here beneath the saw-toothed dome of time.

In these scattered observations I have touched on only a handful of these shorter untitled pieces translated by Vyt Bakaitis. Without further commentary, I will leave you with one last poem, giving in this way the last word, as I should, to Jonas Mekas:

Seared in the sun's heat,
these bleak, pallid white
bushes of lilac
skim past your eyes
in heaps, grown to hills
sunflower crowns have filled
to ripeness,

it's August
stacked the plots, in fields
of rock,
it's history and
blood that is so
near, it seems, if you
lay hand to it
the red will
start streaming
from fields of
sunflower
yellow.

Endnotes

1 *The Story of a Life*, translated by Aloma Halter (New York: Schocken Books, 2004).
2 *Blooms of Darkness*, tr. Jeffrey M. Green (NY: Schocken, 2010).
3 *The Story of a Life* 125.
4 *The Story of a Life* 103.
5 *The Story of a Life* 158.
6 *The Story of a Life* 58-59.

BENJAMIN SLOAN lives in Charlottesville, VA. *The Road Home*, a chapbook of his poems, is available from Thirty West Publishing House.

"At work early in the morning someone talking on a phone down an echoey hallway is too far away to puzzle out individual words, but the voice's melody —alternating with periods of silence standing in for the other half of the conversation—suggests an upbeat trend that, mixed with trucks and motorcycles on a nearby interstate, gives me hope."

Lee Ann Brown & Louise Landes Levi

Words for a Poet Filming /
  Words
Down
 the
  Page

Lee Ann Brown & Louise Landes Levi Write to Each Other About the Poetry of Jonas Mekas:

April 15, 2018
Addenbrooks Hospital, Cambridge, England

Dear Louise,
Thanks for sending joyful healing images
and words!
Images and words compliment each other in profound
and mysterious ways—even when so "simple" . . .
Have you read Jonas Mekas's poetry?
I have primarily encountered his poems at annual
Poetry Project New Year's Day Marathon Readings.
I've heard he's got a vast "living archive" out in Brooklyn
And of course there's Anthology Film Archives
One of my favorite movie theaters—
I call it the Poetry Project of Film
It's where, in my early twenties on first arriving in the City, I first saw his intertitled home movies documenting daily occurrences like poetry rock band the Fugs meeting in an East Village restaurant and children in brightly colored raincoats running down 2nd Avenue in city rain contrasted with Kodachrome shots in green:
Maybe that made me know children were
Possible for me in the city
Possible for me to "have" them here

Play being possible on a city Avenue
And the Diary Film became a possibility, an aspiration.

As poets writing to each other around another poet's work I ask for the permission to write in responsive poetry:

Two Attempts at Memory of *DIARIES, NOTES AND SKETCHES AKA WALDEN* by Jonas Mekas

The new made nostalgia of a window lit up at night against a blue black sky
Kodachrome green rainbows against the grass with 2 kids contrasting down 2nd Avenue "home movies" of the new extended family I am electing—the family of poets! However dysfunctional it will turn out to be that they are my family—the meeting of the Fugs in a restaurant—maybe Christine's—now gone—I started making my own films in word and image but wanted them to be in the avant-garden of single-framing so as to "estrange" reality—but then I saw the beauty of "clear style" to show the extreme diapositive of the daily moment—shadows of trees with something sinister behind the way we sat in the garden behind the restaurant—hot sun sheltered by love / Jonas Mekas poetry's—like a film strip / deep everyday life consciousness / in film / filming parallel writing / Editing parallel to making poetry / Sometimes each shot is like a word or phrase or line / edited disjunctively / could be a kind of poem / or serially in sections unfurling / or sketches / studies of what's going on that can be rearranged / a poem or a film / I think this is key in writing about Jonas Mekas's Poetry / which I will write to You about now, Louise, as sister world traveler poet composer, one rooted and passing through the wild past of Lower East Side

Love, Lee Ann

Dear Lee Ann: April 2018, Bagnore, Italy

strange, I keep thinking of Jonas these days—I was/am
a friend of last great love of his or acolyte, a French
filmmaker—she sublet my room

in Brooklyn, made a film in the loft, connected
to Jonas, later went to Japan w. him, film showing at
Archives—et. al. He said he fixed his teeth for her, so he
cld. kiss her, probably only half in jest ... I never kissed

my (?)/ don›t know what he was, friend, healer,
provocateur (?)—but anyway, need to fix lower jaw,
even if homeless I want good teeth, yes to kiss & also to
chew apples, etc., so hearing Jonas› voice in my
head, just realized a few days ago I HAD to

do it, also I heard his last reading in NYC,
at RED BULL, love poems, it was fantastic, the reading-
I expected a frail voice, no he was powerful …I think that
was last August, just before fateful flight. I'll read thru
the poems, they were sent to gmail which I never
check, not even sure I can get into account,

see you soon, practicing to pass through gates

Love, Louise

Dear Louise

This first poem in Mekas's sequence *Daybooks 1970–1972,* it brings me to that immediacy and fresh intimacy in fall rain I felt watching that first film of his:

I sit
    drink my beer
look out the window

it's raining

newspaper on head
    a man
        runs by
woman
a green raincoat

red street
    crossings

sidewalk
    weaving
    wet

Mekas's short line breaks unfurl like a roll of film or like watching a film; they unfurl in time down the page, the reader's eye the illuminating projector. The short lines share the form with the likes of New York School, such as his neighboring poet Eileen Myles living one street over on 5th Street across the graveyard whose practice echoes that of the great poet of daily living, Jimmy Schuyler. To capture the everyday "shot" of no-ideas-but-in-things. Words unreel, unroll down the page like a ribbon of thought, or interior speech.

This reminds me of my own early poem written around the same time I first saw Mekas's films (circa 1987) and was trying out the "I do this I do that" daily aesthetic style of the "New York School" poets: imbuing simple, everyday documentary of encounter entwined with thoughts that arise, memory and emotion. I remember writing it in a restaurant on 2nd Avenue, the same Avenue Mekas documents so well in his poetic Diary films, the 2nd Avenue Frank O'Hara details so wildly in his long poem of the same name: the long packed Avenue which connects the Poetry Project at 2nd Avenue and 10th Street with Anthology.

Here's one of mine that parallels Jonas's poem quoted above.

Oshinko

I sit too close
To the couple talking

This learning
to be alone
goes on & on
like rain represented
by straight black lines

Jonas Mekas's work embodies the energy I felt hungry for when I first arrived in New York City and saw his work: to admit the personal and the local into poetry and film. To let those small immediate details be central to the work is to let everyday life be a prism for emotion or memory to shine. I identify with the loneliness he feels when he writes later in the sequence, a loneliness so intense it can be visualized like the "straight black lines" in a print by Hokusai, such as "The Bridge at Edo in the Rain" which may have been hanging on the wall in the restaurant I was in, or simply hanging in my mind. Jonas Mekas has a strong sense of the intersection of visual and verbal: it's almost as if he was talking to himself in pictures.

In my first book *Polyverse*, I sought, as Bernadette Mayer challenged, to "write in as many ways as you can imagine." One of those ways is the straightforward, imagistic, diaristic, "I do this I do that" poem which privileges everyday details and a sense of the notational on the fly. I find these elements at work in the poetry of Jonas Mekas and I can't help but think of his poetic practice as deeply enmeshed with his film diaries. These parallel practices in different mediums become complimentary, each standing on its own, but with possibilities of intersection. Both practices relish quotidian detail: such as in Section 9 of Daybook

> Times were bad.
> Now, everything
> -'s gone in
>   the past.
>
> But one
> pain
> stuck,
> from
> across
> the lake.
> — — —
> P.S.
> One detail:
>
>   Father shoved up against
> a wall,
> I lie
> face to the ground.
>
> White potato

blossoms.

A personal window into the horror of history.

Much has been written about the "poetic film" of the '60s, and at the same time, not enough has been written about the parallels and divergences of this aspect of the "New American Cinema" and what has been termed the "New American Poetry" of the '60s, as exemplified by Donald Allen's anthology of the same name that brought together prime figures of the New York School with figures of the San Francisco Renaissance and Black Mountain College. A more thorough study of that would of course hinge on Stan Brakhage's relationship with the work of Gertrude Stein. Brakhage first aspired to be a poet, while living as a young man in the San Francisco basement of poet Robert Duncan and collagist and painter Jess Collins, and Jonas Mekas is the only filmmaker of the era who had an equally developed poetry practice alongside his filmmaking. He can be seen as a hinge figure who has an actual parallel practice of filmmaking and poem-making.

There is an intense documentary aspect to the poems that is interlaced with the films—in his film diaries, and Mekas intercuts thoughts with cinematic embodiments of perception of the present moment. His intimate and fearless portrait of events around the death of poet Allen Ginsberg bear witness to the unfolding of those days and to another relationship with the poetry "of the neighborhood." Allen, who was fascinated with the present moment—with being in the "now" of life—excitedly called up many friends as he was dying and would have loved that Jonas did his best to document what happened as he passed through the Bardo in his video "Scenes from Allen's Last Three Days on Earth as a Spirit."

See: http://jonasmekas.com/online_materials/#scenes_from_allens_last_three_days_on_earth_as_a_spirit

I was surprised to see myself briefly in the lobby of Allen's funeral at the Shambala Center on 22nd Street holding a video camera myself!

Love, Lee Ann

Addenbrooks again

Dear Louise

The woman next to me is sitting up first time in a month after a car accident

She is saying wow at the green hills we can see out the window

Yesterday it was total fog over the hills and today it's clear

Now she's standing in a Frame and saying wow her face is glowing

Since it's about being where one IS and making poetry in the here and now and seeing how it connects to whatever else I am thinking about—I catch the poem of wonder on the fly and I write this from my adjacent hospital bed where I am awaiting an operation on my extravagantly broken ankle:

Proprioception to One's Own Garden

for Fiona, next bed over,
Addenbrooks Orthopedics Ward

Being the sixth sense you need and will have again
Connecting nerves and muscles in balance movement thought

When you first saw the green hills out the window
I saw your eyes fly open in wonder

A little start of electricity sprang up around the room

To all who witnessed you stand up
For the first time in a month
Here's the ode to that

Proprioception is one of the words poets love
Since it provides a big touch interface of the way
We move around the world—describes how
Sensory nerve fibers are actually spiraling around
Muscle Spindles in a delicate tapestry of sensation

Restoring the sense of touch to fluid movement
The perception of touch actually takes place in the brain
Not in the hand itself
If you watch any child   they put their hand in the mouth
They are connecting their own sensations

Proprius is Latin for own
As in property, proprietary, appropriation
Reception as in receiving
From capere—to capture to grasp
One's own taking of the gifts around us

So like Virginia Woolf talking about the importance of having a
Room of One's Own   In this case it's our own body's gift
That we inhabit it
We are it
and it will miraculously tend towards self integration again
On a beautifully intricate subconscious level

We will not take for granted

++++

/// How would I "film" this /// as a poem?
How would I make a poem film?

++++

Moving in Proprioceptive dance, Jonas Mekas as handheld poet of film moving through his life filtering his existence into unspooling diaries of image—thought— flow

+++++++

In Mekas's serial long poem "Words Apart"
The first section is "Images"
The whole length of it
looks and acts like an epic film
of moments
passing through a gate in that
it proceeds down the page
in time
like a strip of film
slipping with sprockets
of consonants down
down the page—
Images flash by
that evoke deep feeling
or melancholic nostalgia
political in the everyday present
of walking down the street
full of lit windows
and shades of trees
moving in urban park wind

Like the earlier *Daybooks*, where Mekas wrote:

> I
> prowl
> and
> prowl
>
> lonesome
> down
> streets
> of words,
>
> just
> waiting for
> someone
>   to take
>   my hand
> and
> lead me
> home.

A solitary figure writes in meta-moments on form and practice:

> I write
> with
> -out any constraints.
>
> Content and form will
> settle
> the field.
>
> Memory

still
keeps bleeding.

In this book-length work, Mekas extends his wanderings into philosophical, existential territory. Once again, the rain returns. Always the atmosphere the words are born into:

2.

Once
again,
it's
raining.

I
lie
here
and
listen

to
rain
drops
breaking

on the
yard

as
though
raining
into

the soul
itself.

3.

The man
sitting

deep in
orchard
shade

is
watching
appletrees
the heat
struck
vibrate

sky
all
trembling
linden.

And then of course, there's the side of Jonas's work springing joyful, imaginative from the rocks of childhood:

> Oh, the scent there is from the thyme-sprigs!
> As I sit on a blue rock, patched with soft moss, with the tiny bugs,
> it all hangs together, all as one—
>
> the people so tiny and small, dancing for me there,

and waving, and laughing, across the blue stones, in a gentle setting of sunlight and moss—so my mother used to say—they are always there, out to greet me—

Ah, how I'd like to be seeing you now, all the little people from my childhood, out on a blue stone, among the thyme-sprigs, that smell, that space—

Love, Lee Ann

July 20, 2018 Amsterdam

LA, it is difficult to write in relation to
film imagery, in Jonas's work, as I don't know
his films that well, but of course did see *Guns*
of the Trees & Hallelujah the Hills,
(Adolfas Mekas) early on, &
Pull My Daisy, which

is Robert Frank's but the 'Mekas' stamp

is upon it. I note the early work is nostalgic, as
if creating a past, whether this actually exists-
ted as depicted was the subject of re-

cent *NY Review of Books* article, but
is that fair—is 'memory,' not a function of our
collective effort to deal w. the inexplicable
passage of time that will eventually

finish memory & each of us. The nostalgic
(I presume) early works are very touching, whether

or not they are invention is not the prerogative-
Idylls of Semeniskiai, he paints for me the journey
I have taken but in (naked) imagination to my
Romanian/Armenian heritage ... an al-
most neo pastoral recollection that, with the advent
of the NYC avant-garde quickly morphs into
a far more experimental form of survival

& a dissociation from the imagined in-
tegrity of the birthplace or place or country of
origin. I recently heard Jonas read, his read-
ing of his own verse more powerful for

me than a casual reading of it, the man
is now 95, flanked by his entourage, of necessity,
I expect at RED BULL a soft voiced elder but
am confronted w. a man of powerful

emotion & a belief in self, in the visionary
dimension of 'self'—totally unexpected in a man of
his demeanor, often seen of course, at the
Anthology & in various photographic
studies, over the years. This de-

termination & this unexpected power may have
been magnified by the presence of his young
protege, from whom there has been the

typical estrangement & whom I had en-
couraged to come to the reading, being a
friend of his. In his later (published) works

Letters, etc., Mekas transforms both his
nostalgia & his experiment w. the formal considerations
of the avant-garde, to write a naturally flowing,
& in the American idiom, NYC based
versification of the present, with

gratitude for that present, in its glory &
its hopelessness. Mekas is not an optimist but
he perceives that which is perceptible as
poetic agency & he does so with abso-
lute humility. *As I move ahead.*
ahead. It is time for a re -

evaluation of his work on paper, having
amused us & assisted us for so
long with the experimental
image in the cinema-
tographic arts,

film as image of the moving world.

My friend, his former protege
writes to me in confusion, did she
expect her mentor to be a saint ?—Mekas
is clearly concerned with himself as
observer, in this sense the same

eye that perceives the imagery he has
recorded on film, in his poetry, manifests
as spontaneous voice, he is not
'creating' imagery but mani-

festing as a poetic voice at the turn of
the Millenium. One wld want to

know more about the women
who inspired him, also active in the
avant-garde of the era, the reportage is
mostly & welcomingly concerned
w. the usual suspects in the

downtown scene, but apart fr. that
consideration, this work is a
study of consciousness,

moving fr. the depth of dislocation
to the discovery of the new land—which
is also a new state—with the
mind of the filmmaker &
a newly discovered
poet, Jonas

*

Today, my birthday, I am reborn in the lights
on the AMSTEL & in the cinematic re-
flections of a poet/filmmaker who

in my earliest adolescence presented

an alternative, a poetic view overcoming
unspoken tragedy & creating new value
& trajectory, new form & we hoped
ardently, if unspoken, as such

a new freedom.

*

Louise Landes Levi 20. July 2018
Amstel River, Amsterdam, NL

Lee Ann Brown adds this postscript:
Sources: *Daybooks: 1970–1972*, which Mekas describes as "Seventy-six poems, I wrote them between 1970 and 1982, in Lithuanian. Vyt Bakaitis translated them into English and they were brought out in 2003. Diaristic, casual poems, all dealing with my life, thoughts and feelings of that period—relaxed and looking ahead optimistically, but still with dark memories lingering in the background—"
(http://jonasmekas.com/poetry/)
Also, *Words Apart and Others*, q.v. in the timeline on page 9 of this book.

LEE ANN BROWN is a poet, filmmaker and singer of "Neo-hymns and Ballads," author of over six books of poetry. She performs her work often in New York City where she edits Tender Buttons Press and teaches at St John's University. In 2017-2018 she was the Judith E. Wilson Poetry Fellow at the University of Cambridge and curated the Polyphonic Poetry Festival where she performed collaborative versions of the songs of William Blake and old-time ballads with Louise Landes Levi in St. Peter's Chapel above Kettle's Yard.

"Passion is to make art the will help show you others the glories of the everyday aura the moment it all clicks in and makes you see the world around you as art. I am scared of the way we are hurtling down the highway the lanes are narrower here hurting themselves on the cow burial class issues are here in more ways than one."

LOUISE LANDES LEVI is a poet, performer, translator and a founding member of Daniel Moore's Floating Lotus Magic Opera Company, America's first fusion orchestra. After receiving a BA, with Honors, from UC-Berkeley, and studying at Mills College with the sarangi-master Pandit Ram Narayan, she traveled alone overland to Afghanistan in the late 1960s and to India, via Istanbul, Tabriz, Mashed, Herat, Khandahar, Kabul, Peshawar, Rawalpundi and Lahore, to research North Indian sangeet (classical music) and its poetic tradition. Several translations followed: René Daumal's classic study of Indian aesthetics, *Rasa, or, The knowledge of Self* (New Directions, 1982); from the Middle Hindi of Mira Bai, an archetypal singer-saint of the 16th century, *Sweet On My Lips: The Love Poems of Mira Bai* (Cool Grove Press, 1997, 2003, 2016); and Henri Michaux's *Toward Totality: Selected Poems* (Shivastan, 2006). She has published more than a dozen books of poetry and autobiographical prose, including most recently: *Crazy Louise OR la Conversazione Sacra* (Station Hill Press,2017), *Love Cantos, 1-5* (Jack In Your Box, 2011); *The Book L* (Cool Grove Press, 2010); *Tower 2/Tara or dc-x* (Il Bagatto, 2009); *Banana Baby*, with facing Italian translations by Alessandro Tuoni (Super Nova, 2006); and *Avenue A & Ninth Street* (Shivastan, 2004). Her electronic chapbooks may be found at the website Big Bridge. Her recordings include most recently: *From the Ming Oracle* (Sloowax, 2014). Her electronic chapbooks & her essay on Francesco Clemente, "Painting, Pilgrimage, Prayer" (Emblems & Mountains, 2012) can be found at www.bigbridge.org. Her recordings include most recently: *Ikiru or The Wanderer* (Oaken Palace, 2018, Big Bridge 19: Home, www.ridge.org). *From the Ming Oracle* (Sloowax, 2014), an instrumental and spoken word compilation of her works from the late sixties to the near present; *City of Delirium* (Sloow Tapes, 2011); and the forthcoming LP *Colloidal Love Poem* (AudioMER.). John Giorno writes: "Her poems sing in the mind and dance through the heart and throat, and arms & legs, w. great clarity and bliss. Louise is Saranswati, goddess of poetry." Levi has studied with such masters as Annapurna Devi, Ali Akbar Khan and La Monte Young. When not performing, she lives in a stone tower in Bagnore, Italy, with winter quarters in New York, her birthplace, and elsewhere.

"**http://www.stationhill.org/authors/louise-landes-levi/**"

Penny Arcade
On Jonas Mekas

I have lived among the giants of contemporary culture, beginning in the late sixties with John Vaccaro, director of the Playhouse of the Ridiculous; H.M. Koutoukas, the playwright; Jack Smith, filmmaker and father of text-based performance art; Charles Ludlam, actor extraordinaire, writer, and director; Peter Hujar, photographer; Andy Warhol, artist and cultural instigator; Taylor Mead, actor and poet; Charles Henri Ford, Surrealist poet and art maker; Judith Malina, actress, writer, poet, activist, and theater maker; and Jonas Mekas, filmmaker and poet. I often refer to these artists as the architects of the counterculture. Over the past fifty years I watched as the forms they brought into being created the current landscape of culture in which we now live and influenced the artistic mediums in which they worked, not only for decades but permanently altering the trajectory of those art forms. Of these artists only two have lived past ninety; two lived into their eighties. Taylor Mead, who died at eighty-eight, had his years of high function slow down considerably after the age of seventy-eight. Judith continued to write, act, and direct up until her death at age eighty-eight. One of the others, Charles Henri Ford, continued to write Haiku and make collages up till his death at ninety-four but had long stopped participating in the outside world. Only one of these artists has been able to ride out nearly a century of artistic development and at ninety-five years is still operating in what I call a developmental arc, which is to say Jonas Mekas continues his investigations unabated by time or age.

We often hear the term "poetry in motion," but Jonas Mekas brings to me the thought of poetry in action, because at his essence, at his impulse, he operates as a poet in all he does, especially in his filmmaking, because there he attempts the improbable, to make poetry without words.

Jonas Mekas is an elemental poet. His work is grounded in nature and in the ephemera of the seasons, of day and night, of snow, wind, rain, sun, of sweat, the grunt of lifting, of physical exertion, of the small thing observed, chapped hands, wet feet, hot bread, sweet wine. Jonas mines the field of memory, in that most misunderstood place, the present, where the past is laid out like a banquet, to be savored and explored, investigated and reinvestigated, returned to again and again, by the light of the moon or the sun, or in the dark, in the spring or the summer, winter or fall, we walk with Jonas, the furrowed ground, the melting snow, the green shoots, breaking through the damp earth, the full canopy of the forest, first green then brown, then bare. The light of dawn or sunset or full sun changes what sits in his unfurling hand, that he motions us, through his words to look at. I must return for a moment to Jonas's age. Particularly now to be of great age is of interest, it would appear, only to scientists, for in our culture, our society today, age is cause for dismissal. Yet they who study human nature and development know that the last part of life contains a most important period, the completion of character, yet so many leave the world before they attain great age, that we do not see many who continue to make art, who continue their developmental arc alongside their completion of character, and it is this rare confluence that Jonas Mekas brings to us. Once he said to me, "I hate that word 'worker.' I once wrote a manifesto against workers, because workers do not love what they do! They do things for money! They will make the needles that go under the fingers, to torture people. Another word I hate is 'retire'; if someone retires, it means they did not love what they were doing. Workers retire." Then Jonas told the story of the sculptor in Lithuania, his birthplace, who died while carrying a stone. Many poets write only during a certain period of their lives. Emily Dickinson, although prolific, wrote the majority of her poems over a thirteen year period, from 22 to 35. We do not have many examples of poets who wrote consistently for the better part of a century. In Jonas we find his inquiry does not change; he is embedded in the loam and earth of his childhood even on the asphalt streets of NYC. Even after seventy-eight years, far from the meadows and forests of his younger life, these are his concerns, nature and that which is unalterable. Like the farmer his birth destined him to be, but transposed by urban circumstance to the growth instead of the ineffable; of beauty, of spirit, of poetry.

In poetry, Jonas, the farmer's son, plants words like seeds, tending the tender shoots, that they might blossom to answers, to solace, to a quieting of questioning. Season after season he returns, to the same crop of his concerns, again to sow and wait and reap only to sow again to wait to reap.

Oh Jonas, I walk the muddy roads with you, take stock of the brush by the wayside. Note the small blue flowers that pinch through the soil. The poems, like the rush of clouds overhead, are on the move. The sky turns pale then blue then indigo. The lamp is lit, then extinguished. The wind sighs against the eaves of the house, the trees croak in unison, your words are like stepping stones through an ancient river bed, where the waters swirl, then ebb, then fall away to a stony, dry, empty place that suddenly wells up with emotions, so simple, so basic, like bread, like milk, like wine. We follow your eye as you follow the raindrop's journey down the windowpane, searching for a completion that never comes whole, no, instead is forever fragmented in the everything of it, like a prism, sending the eye in different, shining directions. The warm sun releases the oil of the thyme shrubs where they grow against the rocks, and we sit with you on a patch of dry grass or a mossy log, our hearts rising with yours, as the sun tickles our eyelashes and golden showers of sun sprinkle down on us from pure, blue cloudless skies. The journey that seemed so long when seen from the starting point folds back on itself when near completion. The stormy sky is so dark but then so bright when the lightning cracks it open, like the poem cracks open our consciousness as your words carry us across the page; we collect your words like children collecting small stones, a talisman of a deeply felt but unknowable mystery, a rite, holy, that we repeat again with each poem.

PENNY ARCADE is an internationally respected writer, poet, performance and theater maker, and an icon of artistic resistance. She is one of the very few artists in the world who practices long-form, text-based performance art, a form of experimental theater that investigates the boundaries between traditional theater and performance. She is the author of twelve full-length theater pieces, hundreds of solo performance pieces, poems, and essays. Her decades-long focus on the creation of community as the goal of performance and her use of performance as a transformative act mark her as a true original in American Theater. A teenage Andy Warhol Factory Superstar, featured in the Warhol/Morrisey film *Women In Revolt*, Penny occupies a unique position in the American avant garde through her long association with the architects of the American counterculture. With her long-time collaborator Steve Zehentner, Penny has co-helmed The Lower East Side Biography Project "Stemming The Tide of Cultural Amnesia," an oral history project that focuses on self-individuation and the rich cultural history of downtown New York that has broadcasted and cybercasted weekly since 1999. www.facebook.com/thelowereastsidebiographyproject, www.pennyarcade.tv, pennyarcade4ever on instagram, pennyarcadesuperstar FB, twitter pennyarcadenyc.

"I am concerned with what it means to be human in the 21st century."

Sparrow
Jonas in Church

On the first day of this year, at the annual Poetry Project Marathon at St. Mark's Church in the East Village of Manhattan, I heard Jonas Mekas read his piece:

> The Edge
> It was on the very edge that he lived. Most of the time he didn't know on which side of the line his existence was: was he in the inner circle or was he in the outer circle; was he rich, or was he poor; was he just alive or was he living. A hair to the left—and he was another; a hair to the right—he was another again. It was that close. Everything depended not on millions (as he used to say) but on one zero, or, rather, on one token: one ride uptown or one ride downtown. When he sat hungry and low, after a long walk downtown, when he had no money for even a token, he didn't know: was this a monk's test or a punishment. Both were equally in his reach. His life was like the many arms of Buddha, he used to say. It always seemed to him that it was he who was the real master of his life: it all depended on which arm he moved. The freest man of them all, linking the inside with the outside, walking on the very edge of nothingness and fullness. Maybe that's what Buddha was all about, he used to say: walking on the very edge of one's existence. But was this edge an abyss or a brim of fullness—that he didn't know and it didn't matter. But he knew and it mattered to him that while he was walking along that narrow rim, with every slightest movement of any of his many arms he could make gestures, gestures of desperation and gestures of ecstasy. So he continued his journey, cutting with the very edge of his life through the Christ's cross, through the Veronica's scarf, through the Buddha's face and through the very heart of the Island of Manhattan.

(Actually, this is a slightly different paragraph, sent to me by Jonas, with the modest notation: "tiny bit improved version." I hope to still be scrupulously editing my paragraphs at the age of 95.)

Of the 143 readers and performers at the St. Mark's Church that day, Jonas was the oldest, the only true connection to the sacred Fluxus movement. His essay had a Lincolnian lilt—similar to Abraham's famous speech at Cooper Union five blocks and 158 years away:

> A few words now to *Republicans*. It is exceedingly desirable that all parts of this great Confederacy shall be at peace, and in harmony, one with another. Let us Republicans do our part to have it so. Even though much provoked, let us do nothing through passion and ill temper. Even though the southern people will not so much as listen to us, let us calmly consider their demands, and yield to them if, in our deliberate view of our duty, we possibly can.

Can you see the similar legalistic style? Both writers clearheadedly, compassionately, address a vexing dichotomy.

Did you notice that Jonas mentioned Veronica's scarf? St. Veronica came upon Jesus on the Via Dolorosa, wiped the blood and sweat off his face with her veil, only to find his image imprinted forever on the cloth. Veronica's veil was the first photograph! (And thus also the ancestor of film, the medium for which Jonas is best known.) My research partner, Eli Tapuchi, explains:

> Veronica's Veil, the ancient relic, is a piece of cloth of incredible lightness and thinness—so thin, it almost doesn't exist! It wavers on the literal (or figurative) edge of existence, just like Buddha.

One of the sentences in Mekas's essay especially struck me. Even as a child, I knew how much: "Everything depended . . . on one token: one ride uptown or one ride downtown."

I was born in Lenox Hill Hospital, on 77th Street, then I went home to Horatio Street, in the southwest of Manhattan, below 14th Street—so far west it was, at that time, not included in Greenwich Village, but rather the quasi-industrial "meatpacking district." When I was four, I moved way north, within Manhattan, almost to the very limits of the island: Dyckman Street (the equivalent of 200th Street). So I began on the Upper East Side—just for a few days—headed downtown, then far uptown.

When I was twelve, my parents began bringing me to Washington Square Park on Sundays, to watch youthful folksingers, and I felt the inebriating air of the world downtown. One of the first records I bought was *Downtown* by Petula Clark (1965):

> When you're alone and life is making you lonely
> you can always go . . . downtown.

At the age of thirteen I bought my first copy of the *Village Voice*, as a connection to the fervent downtown life. Each week thereafter I read "Movie Journal," a column by Jonas Mekas in the *Voice*—though I usually couldn't completely understand it. For example:

> Piero Heliczer's evening, *The Last Rites*, was a ceremony, a ritual—really, the most successful (as ritual) of the six rituals presented at the festival. This was not because Heliczer had for his script the New Testament; not because he played a bishop; but because of a certain unfaked directness, immediacy that he produced. Although he was 'acting,' there was something very real about it. Angus McLise's music helped much to sustain this mood . . .

(That was from a November 18, 1965 review of the New Cinema Festival at the Film-Makers' Cinematheque.) Reading Jonas was like receiving postcards from a friend who had disappeared into a baffling country, a nation without even a name. Yet this fanciful landscape Jonas described was just one subway token away . . . .

SPARROW is attempting to single-handedly revive the long-forgotten 1970s hippie delicacy, Lentil Loaf. His latest book is *On certain nights everyone in the USA has the same dream* (Inpatient Press, 2018).

"I'm trying to imagine Taoist Marxism."

Rail Editions, the press imprint of the *Brooklyn Rail*, publishes books of art and literary criticism, poetry, experimental fiction, prose meditation, artists' writings, and works in translation.

ISBN-13: 978-0-9907881-5-7
First English Edition, 2018

Rail Editions
253 36th Street, Unit 20
Brooklyn, NY 11212
www.brooklynrail.org

Editor: Vyt Bakaitis
Design: Mike Tully
Typefaces: Lars, Adobe Garamond Pro
Printing: Thomson-Shore, Inc.

Small Press Distribution, 1341 Seventh Street
Berkeley, CA 94710 | 800-860-7553
orders@spdbooks.org | www.spdbooks.org

Special thanks to: Gražina Michnevičiutė, Justė Kostikovaitė, Grayson Wolf, John Cappetta, Deena ElGenaidi, Charles Schultz, and Phong Bui.